Ann Peckham

The complete English Cook

Prudent Housewife

Ann Peckham

The complete English Cook
Prudent Housewife

ISBN/EAN: 9783742814210

Manufactured in Europe, USA, Canada, Australia, Japa

Cover: Foto ©Gila Hanssen / pixelio.de

Manufactured and distributed by brebook publishing software (www.brebook.com)

Ann Peckham

The complete English Cook

THE
Complete English COOK;
OR,
PRUDENT HOUSEWIFE.

BEING

An entire new Collection of the most general, yet least expensive RECEIPTS in every Branch of

COOKERY and GOOD HOUSEWIFERY.

With DIRECTIONS for

Roasting,	Fricaseys	Potting,
Boiling,	Pies, Tarts,	Candying,
Stewing,	Puddings,	Collaring,
Ragoos,	Cheese-Cakes,	Pickling,
Soups,	Custards,	Preserving,
Sauces,	Jellies,	Made-Wines, &c.

Together with Directions for placing Dishes on Tables of Entertainment. And many other Things equally necessary. The Whole the meanest Capacity, and far more useful Book of the Kind extant.

In cooking Fowl, or Flesh, or Fish,
Or any nice, or dainty Dish,
With Care peruse this useful Book,
'Twill make you soon a perfect Cook.

By ANN PECKHAM,

Who is well known to have been for Forty Years past noted Cooks in the County of York.

LEEDS:
Printed by GRIFFITH WRIGHT, M,DCC,LXVII.
And Sold by
The Author, and J. OGLE, in Leeds; and Messrs. ROBINSON and ROBERTS, in Pater-noster-Row, London.

THE
PREFACE.

THE following collection of receipts in the art of Cookery, the result of above forty years practice in the best families in and about LEEDS, is not stuff'd with a nauseous hodge-podge of French kickshaws; and yet the real delicacies of the most sumptuous entertainments are by no means neglected.

Sufficient assistance, perhaps more than is always needed, is given the wealthy and hospitable to furnish out their tables on the most uncommon occurences, whilst a special attention is paid to the ordinary occasions of life.— And the middling and lower ranks are instructed how to set off what they have to set before their friends, or for their own use in the neatest manner, and to the best advantage.

A due regard is had throughout to elegance and oeconomy, and most especially to what is nourishing and wholesome, both in the choice and in the preparation of such provisions as the different seasons of the year afford. And proper directions are given for placing any variety or number of dishes upon a table.

The several receipts in pickling, preserving, &c. are given with all possible perspicuity, and in the neatest and cheapest way, and according to the prevailing taste, and the newest fashion. And so much may be said for the present fashion, that it will be found upon trial in various articles

cles lefs expenfive than what is difus'd. Infomuch that the book, it is not doubted will compleatly anfwer the title it affumes, that of the PRUDENT HOUSEWIFE.

The moft accomplifh'd houfe-keepers, will have at leaft the fatisfaction of feeing their own methods approv'd by one who is generally allow'd to be a competent judge, whilft they who have had lefs experience, will meet with fuitable directions how to proceed in all cafes with propriety and reputation.

Such miftreffes as think it a burden to be continually dangling after their maids in the kitchen, may be exempted in a great meafure from that trouble, by putting thefe rules into the hands of their fervants; for fpecial care is taken to make every thing eafy and intelligible to the meaneft underftanding. And it is certain, that the directions which may be read with coolnefs and deliberation at a leifure hour, will more eafily be retained in the memory, than thofe that are given in the hurry of bufinefs from the mouth of the moft refpectable miftrefs.

After all, if there be any fo generous as to encourage the work, out of pure good will and kindnefs to me, almoft worn out in the fervice of the kitchen, they have a fpecial claim amongft the reft of her friends and benefactors, to the grateful acknowledgment, of their moft

Obedient, and moft oblig'd humble Servant,

A. PECKHAM.

THE
Compleat English COOK, &c.

1. *To make* Brown Gravy.

SET a kettle on the fire with a gallon of spring water, put in the scrag-end of a neck of mutton, a knuckle of veal, let it boil and skim it; then put in a little mace, an onion, whole pepper and salt; when it is half wasted, take a stew-pan and rub it with butter over your stove; then take part of a shoulder-piece of beef, slice it, lay it in, and brown it on both sides; then take a little of your broth into your pan, and cut the beef to let the gravy out; and when you have browned all your beef, and you find all the goodness is boiled out, strain it thro' a hair sieve into a bowl.

2. To make WHITE GRAVY.

Take a knuckle of veal, put it into a kettle with as much river water as will cover it, let it boil, and skim it well; then put in whole mace and white pepper, an onion, and a little salt, and boil it 'till all the goodness is out of the meat; then strain it for your use.

3. To make VERMICELLI SOOP.

Take a knuckle of veal, the scrag-end of a neck of mutton, put them into a kettle with as much water as will cover them, a bit of lean ham, and an onion; let it boil, and skim it well, and put in a little mace and salt; when the meat is boiled down, strain it, put it into your clean kettle, and skim the top clean off; then put in two ounces of vermicelli, let it have a boil, and then pour it into your terreen. You may throw in the top of a French roll, if you chuse.

4. To make ONION SOOP.

Take four or five large onions, peel and boil them in milk and water, till tender, changing the water three times in the boiling; then beat them in a marble mortar to a pulp, rub them thro' a hair sieve, and put them into good gravy; fry a few slices of veal and lean bacon, beat them in a mortar as fine as forcemeat, which put into your kettle with the gravy and onions, and boil them; mix a spoonful of flour with a little water, and

and put it into the foop to keep it from running; ftrain it thro' a cullender, and feafon it to your tafte; put into your difh. a little fpinage ftewed in butter, and a little crifp bread; ferve it up hot.

5. *To make* CRAY-FISH SOOP.

Take a knuckle of veal, and part of a neck of mutton, put them in a kettle with as much water as will cover them, an onion, a little whole pepper, and falt to your tafte, let it boil; then take twenty boil'd cray-fifh, beat them in a mortar, adding a little of the foop, ftrain and put them into your kettle, with two or three crufts of white bread to thicken the foop; boil two of the fmalleft cray-fifh, and put them whole into the terreen, with a little crifp bread. You may make lobfter foop the fame way, only add to the foop the feeds of the lobfter.

6. *To make* GREEN PEASE SOOP.

Take a knuckle of veal, and part of a neck of mutton, and make of them a little good gravy; take half a peck of young green peafe, boil and beat them to a pulp in a marble mortar; then put to them a little of the gravy, and ftrain them thro' a hair fieve to take out all the pulp; put all together with a little falt, whole pepper, and a quarter of a pound of butter; let it have a boil; then put it into your terreen, and have ready a gill of young peafe boiled to put in.

A 2   7. *To*

7. To make HARE SOOP.

Cut your hare in small pieces, wash it, and put it into a kettle, with a knuckle of veal, and a gallon of water, a little salt, mace, an onion, a few sweet herbs and some crusts of bread; let it stew 'till the gravy be good; fry a little of the hare to brown the soop, and put it into your terreen, with stewed spinage and crisp bread.

8. To make CUCUMBER SOOP.

Take a piece of lean beef, and part of a neck of mutton, a little whole pepper, an onion, and a little salt, let it boil 'till the goodness be out of the meat; then slice some raw beef, and brown it in a stew-pan, with a little butter; put your broth to it, and let it have a boil; strain it, and take off the fat; then take eight middling sized cucumbers, and slice them, but not too thin, boil them in salt and water, and drain them: when you serve it up, put in the cucumbers.

9. To make GRAVY SOOP.

Take part of a shoulder piece of beef, a knuckle of veal, a little salt, an onion stuck with four cloves, boil them in two gallons of water 'till half is wasted; cut three pounds of lean beef in slices; then take a stew-pan with a little butter, shake it in your pan 'till it be hot; then lay in your beef to brown, putting a little of your broth to it, cut it to let out the gravy, put it into your kettle, and let it have a good boil; then strain it, and skim

off

off the fat; take some sellery, and cut it an inch long, boil it in salt and water, drain it, and put it into your soop when you serve it up.

10. *To make* ALMOND SOOP.

Your stock must be made of veal and fowl; then blanch and beat a pound of Jordan almonds very fine, in a marble mortar, with the yolks of six hard eggs, putting in a little cold broth sometimes; put in as much broth as you think will do; then strain it off, and put in two small chickens seasoned lightly with salt and mace, and serve it in a dish; beat up some whites of eggs, and lay it on a sieve to drain: You may put a little of the red colouring in half of it, and lay round the edge of your dish with the point of your knife for garnish.

11. *To make* RICE SOOP.

Take a quarter of a pound of rice, pick and wash it, boil it in veal broth 'till it be very tender; then put in a young fowl, seasoned with salt and mace, adding a pint of cream and the crumbs of a French roll, and serve it up with the fowl in the middle.

12. *To make* VEAL SOOP *with* BARLEY.

Your stock must be a fowl, a knuckle of veal, and some mutton, seasoned with mace and salt; when boiled, then strain it, and put in half a pound of French or pearl barley, boil it an hour; and when you serve it up, put in chopped parsley.

13. *To make* MUSHROOM SOOP.

Your stock must be made of veal, and a little mutton, seasoned with mace and salt; put in a few white-bread crusts, and strain it; have ready some stewed mushrooms to put in when you serve it up.

14. *To make* SOOP MEAGRE.

Set on a kettle of water, put in some crusts of bread, all sorts of herbs, a little salt and butter; boil it an hour and a half; then strain it thro' a sieve. This will serve to make le rice soop, artichoke soop, and asparagus soop.

15. *To make* PEASE SOOP *for* LENT.

Boil a quart of split pease in a gallon of water, 'till they are soft to press thro' a sieve; then put in an onion, a quarter of a pound of butter, a little pepper and salt; have ready a little sellery boiled tender to put in, and some bread cut in dices and fried; so serve it up hot.

16. *To make* BROTH *for a* SICK PERSON.

Take a leg of veal and put it into a kettle with a gallon of water, let it boil, and skim it very well; put in three quarters of a pound of currants, half a pound of prunes, a handful of burridge, an handful of mint, and an handful of heart's tongue; let them simmer together 'till all the strength be out of the meat, then strain it. If you think the person be in a heat, put in violet leaves and suttery.

17. *To*

17 *To make* Cake-Soop *to carry in the Pocket.*

Take a leg of veal, strip off the skin and the fat, take the flesh from the bone, and put it into a kettle with as much water as will cover it, and let it boil to a strong jelly; then strain it thro' a sieve, and let it settle; fill some cups with jelly taken clear from the settling; then set on a stew-pan with water, and let your cups in, let the water boil till the jelly becomes as thick as glue; take it out and let it stand to cool, then turn it out of the cups on a piece of new flannel which will draw out all the moisture; turn it once in six hours, and put it on a fresh piece of flannel, and continue to do so till it is dry, and keep it in a dry place; this will make it as hard as glue in a little time. When you use this, boil a pint of water, and pour it on a piece of the cake the bigness of a walnut, stirring it with a spoon till it dissolves, and it will make strong broth; as for the seasoning part, every one may add as they like it; if they were to put any in before, it would make it mouldy; but take care to boil the spice or herbs in the water to be poured upon the cake, and make it savoury to the palate; a dish of good soop may in this manner be made, only let the proportion of the cake answer the above direction. If gravy be wanted for sauce, double the quantity may be used that is prescribed for broth or soop.

20. *To*

19. *To make* CAKE SOOP *of* BEEF.

Take a leg, or what they call in some places, a shin of beef, prepare it as above for the leg of veal, and use the part only as directed in the foregoing receipt, and you will have a beef-glue, which is good for flesh, fish, or fowl sauces.

20. *To make* MUTTON BROTH.

Take a neck of mutton six pounds weight, cut it in two, boil the scrag in a gallon of water, skim it well, then put in sweet herbs, an onion, and a little toasted bread; when it hath boiled an hour, put in the other part of the mutton, a turnip, and a little salt: If you boil turnips for sauce, do not boil them all in the broth, it will make them too strong.

21. *To make* CALF'S HEAD SOOP.

Take a calf's head, clean it, and boil it tender, strain off the liquor, and put into it a bunch of sweet herbs, an onion, mace, salt, and pearl barley, let it boil, and when it's enough serve it up with the head in the middle, boned; garnish with bread toasted brown, and grated round the brim.

22. *To make* OYSTER SOOP.

Your stock must be made of fish; then take two quarts of oysters, scald and beard them, take the hard part of the oysters from the other, and beat them in a mortar, with ten hard yolks of eggs; put in some good stock seafon'd with pepper, salt, and nutmeg; then
thicken

thicken your foop as thick as cream, put in the reft of your oyfters, and garnifh with oyfters.

23. *To make* HODGE PODGE.

Take fome of the lower end of a brifket of beef, cut into pieces two inches long and broad, put them in cold water, blanch them into a pot with carrots, turnips, onion, fweet herbs, and a little of the lean part of a ham, feafon with pepper and falt; let it ftew cover'd clofe, then add to it a little good broth, and let it boil well. You may cut your carrots and turnips in dices, or fcoup them, which you pleafe, and may add a quart of green peafe boiled.

24. *To make* SOOP *without water.*

Take fome beef, cut in flices, or a leg of mutton, feafon it with a little pepper and falt, cut three middling turnips in round pieces, and three fmall carrots fcraped and cut in pieces, a handful of fpinage, a little parfley, a bunch of fweet herbs, and two cabbage lettices; cut the herbs pretty fmall, lay a row of meat and a row of herbs, put the turnips, carrots, and an onion at the bottom of the pot, and lay at the top, half a pound of butter, and clofe up the pot with coarfe pafte; then put the pot into boiling water, and let it boil four hours, or in a flow oven all night; when it is enough, ftrain the gravy from the meat, fkim off the fat, then

put

put it on your dish, with some toasts of bread, and a little stewed spinage, and serve it up.

25. *To make* POTTAGE *without the Sight of* HERBS.

Mince several sorts of sweet herbs very fine, viz. spinage, scallions, parsley, marygold-flowers, succory, strawberry, and violet-leaves, beat them in a mortar with oatmeal; then strain them with some of your broth; boil your oat-meal and herbs with mutton, put in salt to your taste, when all is enough, serve it up on sippets.

26. *To dress* SALMON.

After having drawn and cleaned your salmon, score the sides pretty deep, that it may take the relish the better, lay it on a napkin, and season it with salt, pepper, nutmeg, onions, and parsley, work them up with half a pound of butter, a few bread-crumbs, and put it into the belly of your salmon, bind a napkin about it with pack-thread, lay it in a fish kettle, put to it a quantity of wine, water and vinegar, sufficient to boil it in, set it over a quick fire; when its enough take up the salmon, unfold the napkin it's in, and lay another in the dish you intend to serve it in, lay the salmon upon it, and garnish with oysters, shrimps, and lemon.

27 *To roast a* SALMON *whole.*

Your salmon being drawn at the gills, stuff the belly with oysters, seasoned with mace and salt, lay it on a dish, skewer the tail in its mouth,

mouth, lay butter over it, and pour a gill of Madeira on the dish, and set it in the oven, basting it to let the gravy drip into it; when its enough, lay it on your dish, and take all the fat off the gravy, add to it a little melted butter, and give it a boil; pour your sauce into your dish, and rip open its belly, that the oysters may go into the sauce. Garnish with lemon.

28. *To boil a jole of* SALMON.

After having cleaned your salmon, lay it on a fish-plate; let your water boil, then put in your salmon with salt and a little vinegar; when its enough, drain and lay 't on your dish; garnish with lemon and parsley; for sauce, use gravy, anchovy, and butter in one boat; and butter, parsley, and fennel in another.

30. *To fry* SALMON.

Cut your salmon in pieces an inch thick, dip them in the yolk of an egg, take some crumbs of bread, chopped parsley, salt and mace, mix them together, and sprinkle over your fish; fry them pretty brown; take them up to drain from the drippings; and when you serve 'em up, garnish with crisp parsley and lemon; for sauce, butter, parsley, and fennel.

31. *To pickle* SALMON.

Cut a salmon into half a dozen round pieces, take the blood out and wipe it with a cloth, boil it in two parts water and one of vinegar; but do not put in the fish till the liquor hath boiled half an hour; when it is boiled enough, take it up and drain it; then put in two quarts of white wine, and two of vinegar, a good quantity of cloves, mace, and whole pepper, boil it half an hour; when your salmon is cold, sprinkle it with salt and pepper, laying a layer of salmon, and another of the spices out of the liquor it was boiled in, to keep for use; let the liquor be quite cold before you pour it upon your salmon. You may bass it, if you chuse, as they do sturgeon.

32. *To make stewed* SALMON.

Cut your salmon in pieces an inch thick, fry them a light brown, drain them from the drip, then take a stew pan, put some strong gravy in and red wine, a little horse-raddish sliced, a bit of chian pepper, work a little butter roll'd in flour to make it of a proper thickness; set it over your stove, stirring it till it be hot, then put your fish in, let it simmer on the edge of your stove till you serve it up. Garnish with beet root and horse-raddish.

33. SALMON *in Cases*.

Take a piece of salmon, skin it and cut it in thin slices, mince some parsley, green onions and mushrooms; put your parsley and green onions into a stew-pan, with some butter, pepper, and salt; then put in your salmon without putting it over the fire again, and toss it up to give it a taste; place your
slices

slices of salmon in a paper-case, put your seasoning upon it, and strew the crumbs of bread over all; let it bake to a fine colour, and serve it up with the juice of lemon.

34. *To boil a* Turbot.

Gut and wash your turbot, and lay it in salt and water, if it be not sweet change the water as you see occasion; then lay it on a fish-plate, and put it into a kettle of boiling water, with salt and a little vinegar, skim it well, and when boiled enough, take it out and let it drain; take off the black skin; lay it on your dish, and garnish with sliced lemon, horse-raddish, and parsley; for sauce, melt some butter, and put into it the meat out of the body of the lobster, the tail and claws cut small, with a little lemon juice, make it hot and pour it into your boat; you must have another boat with butter and parsley; make your dish hot over boiling water.

35. *To fry* Turbot.

Slice your turbot, hack it with a knife as if it were ribb'd, dip it in the yolk of eggs, dredge it with bread crumbs, a little chopped parsley, and a little salt; fry your fish brown, and drain it; garnish with crisp parsley and lemon. For sauce, parsley and butter in one boat; and anchovy, gravy, and butter in another.

36. *To souse a* Turbot.

Draw, wash, and clean your fish from the blood and slime, put it into water and salt
boil-

boiling hot, let it boil gently, and skim it well as it boils; when the liquor hath wasted a little, put in some white wine and vinegar, lemon peel, four cloves, and a little mace; when boiled enough, let it stand till it be cold; put in a lemon cut in slices; take up the fish, put it into an earthen pan, pour on the liquor it was boiled in, and close it up.

37. *To dress* Infant Turbot.

After having cleaned your fish, take the black skin off, score it in diamonds, rub it over with the yolk of an egg and bread crumbs, dredge it with a little mace and salt, fry it crisp, drain the drip from it, and garnish with crisp parsley and lemon; oyster sauce in one boat, and butter and parsley in another.

38. *To bake a* Turbot.

Lay some butter in a dish, the size of your turbot, lay it on, and season it with salt, pepper, and nutmeg; rub it over with melted butter, and dredge it with bread crumbs; put to it a pint of white wine, and bake it in the oven; when enough, lay it on your dish, skim the fat from the liquor it was baked in, and put to it a little melted butter, and an anchovy; pour it into your boat, and garnish your dish with shrimps and mushrooms.

3 . *To boil a* Cod's-Head.

Clean the head very well, rub it with salt, and lay it on a fish-plate, having ready your

your fish-kettle with boiling water and salt, put in your fish, when it is enough, take it up to drain, and take off the skin, lay it on your dish, and garnish with oysters, lemons, and barberries. You may have lobster, oysters, or shrimps for sauce.

40. *To crimp* Cod.

Take a gallon of well-water, put in a pound of salt, boil it half an hour, skim it well, then put in your slices of cod; when they are enough, take them up to drain, serve with raw parsley and oily butter in a boat.

41. *To stew* Cod.

Take your cod and lay it in thin slices in a dish, with a pint of gravy, and a gill of white-wine, some oysters, and their liquor, a little mace, salt and pepper; let it stew till it be almost enough; then thicken your gravy with a piece of butter, rolled in flour; let it stew a little longer; serve it hot with sliced lemon.

42. *To boil* Cod Zoons.

Let them lay in hot water a few minutes, then take them out and rub them well with salt to take off the skin and black dirt; when they look white, put them in water, and give them a boil; take them up to drain, dredge them with flour, pepper, and salt; then broil them; for sauce, butter and mustard in a boat.

43. *To fry a* Cod's *Tail*.

Split your tail up by the bone, cut it in
square

square pieces, rub it over with egg, and dredge it with bread crumbs, shread parsley and a little salt; fry it brown, then drain, and serve it with crisp parsley, and lemon, and anchovy sauce in a boat.

44. *To stew* Carp *brown.*

Scale and clean them, fry them brown on both sides, take them up to drain, then take a stew-pan, and put in as much gravy and red wine as will cover them, put in some anchovies, and sliced horse-raddish, a little chian pepper and salt, a lump of butter worked in flour, put it into the gravy to make it of a proper thickness, then set it on your stove, and when hot, put in the carp, let it simmer on the stove till you serve it up, take them up with a slice, and pour your sauce on them thro' a hair-sieve. Garnish with scraped horse-raddish.

45. *To stew* Carp *white.*

Scale and clean them, save the roes and milts, stew them in some good veal gravy, seasoned with mace and salt, and a glass of madeira; thicken your sauce with a little butter and flour, and serve it hot. Garnish with the roes, milts, and parsley.

46. *To broil* Carp.

When your carp is cleaned, lay it on the gridiron, and when one side is enough turn it over; make your sauce of butter, anchovy, capers and lemon, a little pepper and salt, and pour it into your boat hot.

47. *To*

47. To boil CARP.

Clean your carp, put it into a pan of boiling water and salt, when it is enough, drain it; make your sauce of gravy, red wine, anchovy, a shallot shread, a little whole pepper, and a blade of mace; then thicken your sauce with butter and flour; serve your carp in a napkin; pour your sauce hot into the boat with a little juice of lemon.

48. To fry LAMPREYS.

Bleed them and save the blood, and wash them in hot water to take off the slime; cut them in pieces, and dredge them with flour; fry them in butter, and put to them a little white wine, salt, pepper, nutmeg, and a bunch of sweet herbs, give them a shake over the stove; then put in the blood and a few capers, and serve it hot. Garnish with slices of lemon.

49. LAMPREYS *with sweet Sauce.*

After having cut them in pieces, take out the string that runs along their backs, fry them with butter and a little flour, till they are brown; then add some red wine, a little sugar, cinnamon, salt and lemon; when they are enough, put in the blood, and give them a turn or two more, so serve them up hot.

50. To boil EELS.

Skin, gut, and wash your eels, cut them in pieces as long as your finger, put them in a pan with as much water as will cover them, with an onion stuck with cloves, a
few

few sweet herbs, a blade of mace, and a little whole pepper; cover them close and set them over your stove to boil gently; when they are near enough, put in a piece of butter rolled in flour, a little salt and shread parsley; so dish them up with the broth.

51. To stew EELS.

Take your eels and cut them what length you please, wipe them dry with a cloth and fry them, drain them from the drip, then take a stew-pan, put in some gravy and red wine, a little horse-raddish, an onion, a little mace, and an anchovy, make them a proper thickness, put in your eels, and let them simmer over your stove; when you serve them up, lay them on the dish, and strain your sauce upon them.

52. To spitch-cock EELS.

Take your eels, skin and wipe them, turn them round, prick a skewer into them to keep them from breaking loose, dip them in the yolk of an egg, season them with pepper and salt, dredge them over with bread crumbs, and set them before the fire to broil. For sauce, butter, gravy and anchovy in one boat; and butter and parsley in another.

53. To boil TENCH.

Take tench from the pond, gut and scale them, set on a stew-pan with water, seasoned with salt, whole pepper, lemon peel, a blade of mace, horse-raddish sliced, and a bunch of of sweet herbs; when they boil put in your tench, and when enough take them up to drain; serve 'em in a napkin. For sauce, gravy, butter and shrimps in a boat.

54. *To stew* TENCH.

Take your tench, clean, and wipe them dry, fry them and drain them from the drip; then take a stew-pan, put in some gravy and red wine, a little horseraddish, an anchovy, a little chian pepper or mace, a piece of butter rolled in flour; make it hot, and put in your tench; and let it simmer over your stove; when you serve it up, strain your sauce thro' a sieve. Garnish with horseraddish and lemon.

55. *To bake* TENCH.

Take your tench from the pond and kill them by giving them a hard stroke on the back of the head, clean them and lay them on a dish with butter over them; put them in the oven, and when they are enough, lay them on your dish. Garnish with lemon and barberries. For sauce, butter, catchup, and gravy.

56. *To stew* BARBELS.

Clean your barbels, put them into a stew-pan, with wine, gravy, salt, pepper, and a bunch of sweet herbs, set them over your stove; when they are near enough, thicken your sauce with butter and flour, so serve them up.

57. *To*

57. To broil BARBELS.

Scale and draw your barbels, score them on the sides, dredge them with flour, and lay them on the grid-iron, turning them while enough; then lay 'em on your dish. For sauce, butter, anchovies, and capers.

58. To boil MULLETS.

You must boil the mullets, and take care of the roes and milts; when they are boiled, pour out part of the water, and put into the rest a pint of red wine, an onion, salt, mace, the juice of a lemon, and an anchovy; boil all these well together, and put in the fish; let it simmer over your stove, and serve it with oysters or shrimps.

59. To broil MULLETS.

Scale and clean them, dredge them with flour and lay them on your grid-iron to broil; make your sauce of butter, capers, pepper, salt, and the juice of orange: serve them hot.

60. To roast a PIKE.

Gut, wash, and dry your pike, make a forcemeat with oysters, sewet, bread crumbs, thyme, parsley, anchovy, mace, salt and eggs, beat in a mortar; then fill the belly and sew it up, turn it round on a dish, lay butter over it, and set it in the oven; when it's half enough, rub it over with egg and dredge it with bread crumbs; then set it in

the

the oven till enough. Garnish with capers and lemon, and make your sauce of butter, gravy and lobster.

61 *To boil a* PIKE.

Take a pike, scale, gut, and turn it round; set on a pan with water, and put in your fish, with a little salt, when it boils; take it up to drain; for sauce, butter, parsley and gooseberries. If it be a large one, three quarters of an hour will boil it.

62. *To fry a* JACK.

Gut, wash and wipe it dry, rub it over with egg, dredge it with bread-crumbs, and fry it. Garnish with crisp parsley, and for sauce, anchovy, gravy and butter.

63. *To crimp* SCATE.

Cut it into long slips cross-ways an inch broad and ten long, more or less according to the bigness of your fish, boil it quick in water and salt; when it is enough, put a drainer upon your dish, and lay it on: for sauce, butter and mustard in one boat; and butter, gravy and anchovy in another.

64. *To dress* FLOUNDERS.

Take off the black skin, score the fish on that side with a knife, and lay them on a dish, pour some vinegar on them, and strew on good store of salt; let them lay half an hour, having ready a pan of boiling water, put into it a little white wine, sweet herbs, and the vinegar wherein they lay; when it boils put in the fish, and when they are enough,

enough, drain them, and serve them up with anchovy, orange and barberries.

65. *To stew* PLAICE.

Gut and wash them, cut off the end of the tails, and put the fish into a stew pan with some gravy, white wine, truffles, mushrooms and morels, the milts, a piece of butter rolled in flour, and a little mace and salt; set them over a stove, and turn them gently for fear of breaking; when they are enough, serve them up with the sauce, white, and sliced lemon.

66. *To fry* PLAICE.

When they are cleaned, wipe them dry, dredge them with flour, and fry them brown; serve them with crisp parsley; or you may broil them on a grid-iron, and serve them with butter and vinegar.

67. *To fry* SOALS.

Gut, wash, and wipe them, take off the black skin, and score the white one in dices; then rub them over with the yolk of an egg, dredge them with bread-crumbs, and fry them crisp; serve them with crisp parsley and oyster sauce in a boat.

68. *To pickle* STURGEON.

Take a sturgeon, gut and clean it very well with salt and water, wiping it very dry with coarse cloths, without taking any of the scales from it; then take off the head, fins, and tail, cut the fish into pieces about four pounds each, take out the bones

as

as clean as you can, and lay the fish a day and night in falt and water; then tie them with bals strings, which will keep the fish close in the boiling; lay the fish on a tin plate the bigness of the pan bottom, with holes in.—*To make the pickle*, Take four gallons of water and one gallon of vinegar, four pounds of salt, and a quarter of a pound of whole black pepper; when it boils, put in the fish, and take care to skim off the oil as it boils, and supply it with hot water as it boils away, or else the sturgeon will be rusty; when it's enough, take it up to drain, and when quite cold, put the fish in clean tubs, cover it with the liquor it was boiled in, and close it for use.

69. *To pickle* SPRATS.

Take the heads of the sprats and salt them a little over-night, the next day lay them in a barrel, with a layer of salt betwixt each layer of sprats, a little lemon-peel and some bay leaves, till you have filled the vessel; then cover it up close, pitch it that no air can get in, and set it in a cool cellar, turning it upside down once a week. They will be fit for use in three months.

70. *To pickle* COCKLES.

Take fresh cockles, wash them, and put them in a pan over the fire 'till they open; then take them out of the shells, put to their liquor some white wine, whole pepper, a little vinegar and mace, put in your

cock-

cockles and let them have a scald, then put them into a jar; let your pickle boil, and when cold pour it on your cockles, and close them up. You may do muscles the same way.

71. *To pickle* Lobsters.

Set on a pan with water and salt, when it boils put your lobsters in, and when boiled, take the meat whole out of the claws and tails. For pickle, take vinegar, white wine, whole pepper, mace and salt, let it boil, and when cold put your lobsters in a pot, pour on your pickle, and cover them for use. You may pickle shrimps the same way.

72. *To collar* Eels.

Take a large eel, skin it, cut off the head, split it down the belly, wash and wipe it, take the bone out and leave the back whole; season it with mace, pepper, salt and sweet herbs, then roll it up and sew it; tie it in a cloth and bind it with a roller, boil it in water, salt, white wine, and vinegar, and a blade of mace; when enough, take it up, and let the pickle boil a little longer, and when cold, put in the eel.

73. *To keep* Anchovies.

You must take anchovies, and cover them two inches thick with bay salt.

74. *To boil* Soals.

Clean your soals, take off the black skin, set on a pan with water, a little white wine, vine-

vinegar, falt, and a blade of mace; when it boils put the foals in, and when they are enough, take them up to drain; ferve them up with parfley and butter.

75. *To roaſt* LOBSTERS.

Set on a pan of falt and water; when it boils, put in the lobſters, and let them boil for fix minutes; then take them up and lay them on a dripping pan before the fire, a quarter of an hour, bafting them with butter; ferve them up with butter in a boat.

76. *To ſtew* LOBSTERS.

Take boiled lobſters, break the fhells, and pick out all the meat; cut the tails in two length way; take a ſtew-pan with good gravy, put in fome morels, trufles, a little mace and falt, and fet it over your ſtove till it be hot; fo ferve it up.

77. *To butter* LOBSTERS.

Take the meat out of the fhells, when boiled cut it fmall, put it into a ſtew-pan, with a little gravy, melted butter, a little pepper, falt, and a fpoonful of vinegar, fet it over the fire 'till hot. You may ferve it in fhells, if you pleafe.

78. *To make* SHAM CRAB.

Take a large crab-fhell, and clean it; then take part of a calf's-liver, boil and fhred it fmall, put to it a little anchovy liquor to give it the fifh tafte, mix with it a little lemon juice, pepper, falt, and a little oil, fill the fhell with it, and ferve it up. You may deceive some people, if you do not put in too much of the anchovy liquor; if you would have it hot, put a little melted butter, and no oil, and serve it up in the shell.

79. *To fry* TROUT.

After having cleaned your fish, wipe them dry with a cloth, rub them over with egg, and dredge them with bread crumbs; fry them crisp, and lay them on your dish with all the tails in the middle, some crisp parsley, and parsley and butter in a boat. After the same manner you may dress grayling, perch, gudgeons, smelts, or a chine of salmon.

80. *To pickle* TROUT.

Clean your trout, put as much water and vinegar into a pan as will cover them; take spice and a bunch of sweet herbs, and when it boils put them in; when they are enough, let them lie in the pickle till you use them.

81. *To make* WATER-SOOCKEY.

Take some of the smallest plaice or flounders, gut and wash them clean, cut the fins off, put them in a stew-pan, with just water enough to boil them in, a little salt, and a bunch of parsley, when they are enough, send them up in a deep dish with the liquor, and parsley and butter in a boat.

82. *To dress* HADDOCKS.

Scale, gut and wash them clean, cut the fins and skin off, take the eyes out, turn them round, and do them all over with egg
and

and bread crumbs, and either broil them before the fire or fry them; serve them with oyster sauce in a boat. You may dress whitings the same way.

83. *To stew* OYSTERS.

When you have taken the oysters out of the shells, give them a scald, but not to boil, if you do it will make them hard; wash them one by one from the grittiness, let your liquor stand to settle; take a stew-pan, put in the oysters, and some of the liquor, a little melted butter, a few bread crumbs, two spoonfuls of cream, and a little mace, so serve them up hot.

84. *To make* OYSTER LOAVES.

Prepare your oysters as above, then take what number of French rolls you think fit, cut a piece out of the top, and take out the crumbs, (take care of the pieces to lay on the tops when they are filled,) clarify half a pound of butter in a pan, soak the loaves well in it till they are crisp, drain them then make your oysters hot and fill them.

85. *To escalop* OYSTERS.

Open your oysters, scald and wash them, butter your escalop shells, and dredge them with bread crumbs, then lay in your oysters, with a little butter over them, cover them with bread crumbs, set them before the fire to brown, and baste them with butter; you may set them on hot coals, and do them with a salamander.

86. *To pickle* Oysters.

Give the oysters a scald in their own liquor, wash and drain them; *for the pickle,* take a pint of white wine, a pint of vinegar, and their own liquor, with mace, pepper and salt, boil and skim it, when its cold keep the oysters in it.

87. *To fry* Oysters.

Let your oysters be large, scald, wash and drain them, then mix an egg and a few bread crumbs, in which dip the oysters, and fry them; they are proper for made dishes.

88. *To boil* Mackarel.

Take your fish and clean it, boil it in salt and water; *for sauce,* use butter, gooseberries, and fennel.

89. *To make* Fish Balls.

Take carp and eel, mince them small together with the same quantity of suet, some sweet herbs, savoury spice, bread crumbs and egg, beat all in a mortar, and make it into balls.

90. *To stew* Muscles.

Wash them clean, boil them in beer and salt, then take them out of the shells, take off their beards, wash them, and look under the tongue for a crab, if you find one, throw that muscle away; take a stew-pan with a little gravy, white wine, a little mace, salt, a few bread crumbs, and a little melted butter, put in the muscles, make them hot, and serve them in escalop shells.

91. *To*

91. *To escalop* SHRIMPS.

Take your shrimps out of their shells, season them with salt and pepper; butter your escalop shells, and put in the shrimps, with crumbs of bread and a little butter, and brown them before the fire.

92. *To stew* PRAWNS.

Your prawns being boiled and picked, put them in a stew-pan with a little gravy and white-wine, season'd with mace and salt, thicken'd with a piece of butter rolled in flour; make them hot, and serve them with a little juice of orange; or you may stew them with butter and cream, and serve them in escalop shells.

93. *To fry* HERRINGS.

Clean your herrings, rub them over with egg, dredge them with bread crumbs, and fry them; having ready, onions peeled and cut thin, fry them a light brown, lay the herrings on your dish, and the onions round 'em, with butter and mustard in a boat.

94. *To broil* HERRINGS.

Clean your herrings, cut off their heads, and wipe them with a cloth, flour and broil them, take their heads, mash them, boil them in beer or ale, with a little whole pepper and onion; let them boil a quarter of an hour, then strain it, thicken it with butter, flour and mustard; lay your fish on the dish, and pour your sauce into a boat.

95. To bake HERRINGS.

Cut off the heads and tails of your fish, wash them and strew them with salt, lay them in a deep glazed pot, with whole pepper and mace; pour as much vinegar to them as will cover them, tie brown paper over the pot, and let them stand all night in an oven.

The Times of the Year, when FISH *are in Season, viz.*

JANUARY.

Golden smelts, graylings, or humbers, green river carps, small roaches, codlings, dabs, Feversham oysters, cods, sea flounders, cockles, Colchester oysters, green weifleet, oysters, holybuts, Coles fish, grey lumps, Milton oysters, red lumps, chars, large river flounders, pike, plaice, small river flounders, and turbot in season most months in the year. Thornbacks, maids, foals, gudgeons, bleaks and grigs in season all the year.

FEBRUARY.

Large river flounders, sea flounders, chars, holybuts, large dace, large roach, salmon trouts, salmon breams, river trout, sea perches, and chubs, the last, if not eaten the same day they are taken, are little worth; they spawn in March.

MARCH.

The month of March is the time when all pond fish are in their greatest perfection, and it may be observed, that both males and females, of all kinds of fish, are best before whole-spawning time, that they are sick and unwholesome for three weeks after spawning. Fish in season this month are, large river flounders, sea crabs, cods, sea flounders, chars, basses, silver smelts, sea tench, Willises, and Kingston's.

APRIL.

Sea crabs; sea cray fish; large river flounders; salmon trout; Thames salmon comes into season in April, and is allowed to be caught till the thirteenth of September; river trout, Hampshire is the chief county for trouts; sturgeon is catched this month in the northen seas, and now and then taken in the Thames, the Severn, and the Tyne; this fish is of a very large size, and is in great esteem when fresh taken, to be cut in pieces of eight or ten pounds to be roasted or baked, and pickled and kept for cold treats, the caveer esteemed a dainty is the spawn of this fish; pilchards come in season this month for the first time; sea crabs continue in season; pond carp in season this month, and most months in the year, except part of May, in the beginning of which they spawn; they increase wonderfully, for they breed three times in the year.

MAY.

Sea crabs, still in season; sea cray fish the same; brown shrimps; shads; guard fish; red mullets; mackarel; white prawns and herings; trouts still in season; escalops in the mackarel season.

JUNE.

Mackarel continue in season, herrings and eels; the eels that are taken in rivers and running waters, are better than pond eels, and ot those, the silver ones are most esteemed; and Chichester lobsters and red mullets continue in season.

JULY.

Red mullets still in season; right anchovies the beginning of this month; cray fish are in season all the year, the best in England are said to be taken in the river Kennet at Hungerford; oysters first come in season the twenty-fifth of this month.

AUGUST.

Lobsters and crabs come in season this month, and hold till Christmas, which is called the first season; and from Christmas to June is called the second season; smear dabs; ruffs; and john dorees.

SEPTEMBER.

Barbels; gurnets; roaches; smelts; mackarel, and herrings.

OCTOBER.

Scotch lobsters; grey mullets; dabs; haddocks; whitings; perches; pilchards and herrings still in season.

NOVEMBER.

Tench and dabs still in season; haddocks; sea cray fish; cods; ling; sprats; codlings; Wellfleet oysters, from this month till January.

DECEMBER.

Codlings; flounders; whiteings; dabs; haddocks; ling; cockles; Colchester chars; muscles; sprats; shrimps; lampreys in season from Christmas to June.

96. *To stew a* Rump *of* Beef.

Take a fat young rump of beef, lard it with bacon, and stuff it with shread parsley, brown it in a stew-pan with butter; have ready a kettle of boiling water, put in your beef, with two anchovies, an onion, a little mace, whole pepper, and a bunch of sweet herbs; stew it over a slow fire four hours, turning it several times in the stewing, and keep it close covered; when your beef is enough, take the gravy from it, thicken it with butter and flour, and put it upon the dish with the beef. Garnish with red beet root; there must be no salt upon the beef, only salt the gravy to your taste.

97. *To stew a* Brisket *of* Beef.

Take the middle part of a brisket of beef, skewer the skin down, lard it with bacon, make a little good broth and put your beef in; let it boil five hours, turning the beef every hour, keeping it close covered; when its enough, take out the bones and take off the under skin; then make a ragoo with gravy, sweet-breads cut in dices, truffles, morels, mushrooms, a little salt, mace and whole pepper; then put in your beef, let it stew half an hour, turning it over some times; serve it up, and pour your ragoo over it.

98. *To force the Inside of a* SURLOIN *of* BEEF.

Lift up the fat with a knife, and take out all the meat close to the bone, chop it small, take a pound of suet, and chop it fine, as many bread-crumbs, a little thyme, salt, pepper, half a nutmeg grated, two shallots shread fine, mix altogether, with a glass of red-wine; then put it into the same place, cover it with the skin and fat, skewer it down and cover it with paper; do not take the paper off till the meat is on the dish; take a jack of red-wine, two shallots shread small, boil them and pour into the dish to the gravy that comes from the meat. Spit your beef before you take out the inside.

99. *To boil a* ROUND *of* BEEF.

Take your beef and skewer it close, stuff it with parsley, and tye it with beggar's-inkle, have ready a kettle of boiling water, with a little oat-meal in it, put in your beef; if a large one it will take four hours boiling, turn it every hour, and when its enough, serve it with roots. Let it lay a week in salt before you boil it.

100. BEEF OLIVES.

Take some slices of a rump or any other part that is tender, beat them with a paste pin, season them with mace, pepper, and salt, make a forcemeat of veal, beef suet, a few bread-crumbs, sweet herbs, a little salt,

salt, pepper and mace, two eggs, mix altogether, and beat them fine; take a lump of force-meat, as big as an egg, lay it on your beef, and roll it up and sew it; do them over with yolks of eggs and bread crumbs, butter a dish, lay them on, and bake them in an oven; when you serve them, cut them in two, length ways, and lay them on the dish with good gravy.

101. *To dress* BEEF-STAKES.

Cut your stakes off the rump, not over thin, flat them with a clever, then lay them on a grid-iron, over a clear fire, turning them till enough, lay them on a hot dish with a little gravy, and sprinkle a little salt on. Garnish with horse-raddish and pickles.

102. BEEF *A-la-mode.*

Take part of a buttock of beef, cut it in two pound lumps, lard them with bacon, season them with mace and salt, brown them, then put them into a stew pan with gravy, enough to cover the meat, put in a bunch of sweet herbs, a little mace, whole pepper and salt, stew them till tender, skim it well, and serve it up hot.

103. *To make* DUTCH BEEF.

Take eight pounds of a buttock of beef without bone, rub it all over with a quarter of a pound of coarse sugar, let it lay two days, then wipe it, take a pint of common salt, a pint of salt-petre, and six ounces of bay-salt beaten, rub it well into the beef, and

and let it lay three weeks, turning and rubbing it every day; then few it up in a cloth, and hang it up in a chimney where wood fire is kept for a month, turning it up fide down every day; when you ufe it, boil it in pump water.

104. *To collar* Beef.

Take part of a bed-piece of beef, as much as you think will make a good roll, fkin it, rub it well with falt-petre and bay-falt, and let it lay two days, turn it twice a day; then feafon it with mace, falt, pepper and fweet-herbs, lay the yolks of fix boiled eggs over it, then roll it up tight, and put it in a cloth, tye it clofe at each end, and bind it with a roller; have ready a kettle of fpring water boiling, put it in, and let it boil till you think its enough, which you may know by opening an end; then wrap it tighter, boil a pickle of falt and water, and when cold put it in, making frefh pickle when you fee it wants.

105. *To bake an* Ox Cheek.

Wafh it clean, take the balls of the eyes out, feafon it with pepper and falt, two onions, put it in an earthen pot, with as much water as will cover it, tie a paper over it, and fet it in an oven all night; when you ufe it, take the bones out, and ferve it hot with toafts of bread.

106. *To bake a* Bullock's Heart.

Clean it and lard it with bacon, make a

stuffing of suet, bread-crumbs, parsley, thyme, anchovy, pepper, salt, nutmeg, and an egg, beat it and put it into the cavities of the heart, skewer a caul of veal over it to keep the stuffing in, lay it on a dish and bake it; serve it with gravy.

107. *To dress* OX PALATES.

Boil your palates tender, blanch them, and cut them in pieces the long way of your palate; then take a stew-pan, put in a little gravy, mace, salt, mushrooms, truffles, and morels, a sweet-bread cut in dices, thicken your gravy a little, put in your palates, and serve them hot.

108. *To pickle* TONGUES.

Take the tongue out of pickle, boil and blanch it, rub it over with egg, and dredge it with bread-crumbs, set it before the fire to brown, and serve it with gravy and currant jelly.

109. *To roast a* NEAT'S TONGUE.

Lay your tongues in spring water, make your pickle of six quarts of water, an ounce of salt-petre, an ounce of salt of prunella, half a pound of bay salt, a pound of common salt, and a quarter of a pound of coarse sugar, boil all these together, skim it clean, when cold clean your tongues, and lay them in, at the full length to be covered; turn them three times a week, and let them lay three weeks. You may either use them out of pickle or hang them.

110. *A* Harrico *of* Mutton.

Take a neck or loin of mutton, cut it into six pieces, season it with pepper and salt, and a little mace, brown them on both sides in a stew pan; put to them some good broth, made of the scrag, and some other meat; put in some diced carrots and turnips, and some stewed lettice, cover it and set it over the stove; when enough, skim off the fat, and serve it up.

111. *To Force a* Leg *of* Mutton.

Take out all the meat leaving the skin whole, take the lean of it and make it into force-meat, to two pounds of meat, put three pounds of beef suet, take out all the skins, shred both very fine, and beat them in a mortar, till you know not the meat from the suet; mix with it four spoonfuls of grated bread, six raw eggs, a few sweet-herbs shred small, pepper, salt and mace, mix them all well together, and put them into the skin again, to be in the same form it was before, and sew it up; if roasted, gravy on the dish; if boiled, oyster sauce.

112. *To boil a* Leg *of* Mutton.

Lard the mutton with lemon peel and beet-root, and boil it; *for sauce,* take a little calf's-liver, boil and beat it in a mortar, with two anchovies and two boil'd yolks of eggs; take butter, gravy and capers, mix altogether, pour it into a boat.

113. *To boil a* Loin *of* Mutton.

Skin and bone your mutton, season it with pepper, salt, mace, and a few sweet herbs shred small, sprinkle them all over it, then roll it up tight, and tie it in a cloth; two hours will boil it, then take it up and cut four slices off the ends, which rub over with egg and bread-crumbs, and brown them; pour gravy on the dish, the roll in the middle, and the slices round. Garnish with capers and mushrooms.

114. *To carbonade a* Breast *of* Mutton.

Take every other rib out of your breast of mutton, skewer it round and boil it, take it up and score it with a knife, then rub it over with egg, and dredge it with bread-crumbs, set it before the fire to brown, and serve it up with gravy, butter, and capers.

115. Mutton *kebobed*

Take a loin of mutton, disjoint it between every other bone, and season it with pepper, salt, and sweet herbs, join them together in the same shape as before, and put them on a small spit; roast them before a quick fire, basting them with butter and what comes from them; when enough, serve them up with gravy.

116. Mutton Maintelow.

Take off the skin of a loin of mutton, cut off the thin part, and the other into flakes, flat them with your clever, and season with pepper and salt; then take as many half sheets of writing-paper as you have stakes, butter them, dip your stakes in butter, dredge them all over with bread-crumbs and sweet-herbs, lay them on your papers and close them up; then lay them before the fire, and baste them, to keep them from browning; when enough lay them on your dish. Your sauce poivrade, take some gravy, a little vinegar, shallot shread to a pulp, and a little pepper and salt, make it hot and pour it into your boat.

117. *To dress* MUTTON RUMPS.

Take half a dozen sheep rumps cut large, turn them round and boil them; when they are enough, take them into a cullender to drain, then take the white of an egg beat to a froth, and do your rumps over with it, dredge them with bread-crumbs; you must do them three times over, and set them to dry every time; then fry them brown; you may serve them with gravy or green peafe.

118. MUTTON COLLOPS.

Take mutton that is stale, but sweet, take off the skins, cut them thin, the bigness of a crown piece, season them with a little salt, pepper, mace, parsley, and an onion shred fine; stir it in among your collops, set your stew-pan over a quick fire, put in a little butter, and keep stirring them all the time; when they are enough, put them into a pot to keep hot; put into your stew-pan a little gravy,

gravy, some morels and mushrooms, made hot, put your collops on the dish, and pour your sauce upon them.

119. *To dry a* LEG *of* MUTTON.

Take a leg of mutton, and rub it with an ounce and a half of salt-petre, an ounce of bay-salt, and a pound of common-salt; let it lie nine days, rub it with the brine every day, then hang it up for three weeks.

120. *To collar a* BREAST *of* MUTTON.

Take a breast of mutton, skin and bone it, rub it with bay-salt and salt petre, let it lay for two days, turning and rubbing it twice a day; lay it flat on your table, sprinkle it over with mace, pepper, salt, and sweet-herbs, roll it up, sew and bind it in a cloth; put it into a kettle of boiling spring water, and let it boil for two hours; take it up and bind it tighter; make a pickle of salt and water, then take it out of the cloth, and put it into the pickle cold.

121. *To roast a* CHINE *or* SADDLE *of* MUTTON.

Take off the skin, and skewer it on again, lay it down to roast; when its near enough, take off the skin, baste, salt, and dredge it. *For sauce*, use stewed cucumber, sellery, or pickles.

122. *To boil a* JIGGET *of* LAMB.

Put your lamb in a cloth, and boil it an hour and a quarter, turn it in the boiling, when its enough, lay it on your dish, pour a little parsley and butter over it. *For sauce*, butter, parsley, and gooseberries, in a boat, and spinage on a plate.

123. *To dress* LAMB STAKES.

Take a loin of lamb, cut it into stakes, flat them with a clever, and rub them over with eggs; season them with pepper and salt, and dredge them with bread-crumbs, and shred parsley, fry them brown. Pour gravy on your dish, and garnish with crisp parsley.

124. *To fry* LAMB STONES.

Give them a set in water, take off the skin, cut them in slices, dredge and fry them brown. For sauce use gravy, butter, and crisp parsley.

125 *To force a* LEG *of* LAMB.

Take all the meat out, leaving the bone and skin whole, chop the meat small, with beef suet, oysters, anchovy, sweet-herbs, mace, pepper, salt, nutmeg, and two eggs, beat them in a mortar, fill the skin with it, sew it up, lay it on a dish, put butter over, and bake it; serve it up with gravy.

126. *To dress* LAMB-PURTENANCE.

Clean the purtenance, boil all but the heart, and when enough, take the liver and lights and mince them, stuff the heart with boiled yolks of eggs, and roast it; put gravy and butter to your minced meat, make it hot and pour it on your dish, laying the head upon it; mix your brains with a little butter, and pour upon the head; then cut the heart in four, and lay it with the head on the dish.

127. *To roast* Lamb.

Take a quarter or chine of lamb, spit and paper it, lay it down to roast, and when near enough, take off the paper, baste, salt, and dredge it. Garnish with orange, mint sauce in a boat; if it be in winter when there is no green mint to get, shread a little green parsley, and rub in a little dry mint to give it the taste; add to it sugar and vinegar.

128. *To ragoo a* Breast *of* Veal.

Take every other rib out of a breast of veal, take the skin off the thin part, turn it round; make a stuffing of suet, bread-crumbs, egg, sweet-herbs, and parsley shread, season'd with pepper, salt, and mace, beat in a mortar, cut a place under the brisket, put in the stuffing, and skewer it down, spit and roast it near enough; then take a stew-pan with some good brown gravy, mushrooms, truffles, and morels, and the sweet-bread cut in dices, put in the veal, and set it over a stove to stew half an hour, turning it; then lay it on your dish, and pour the ragoo over it.

129. *To ragoo a* Breast *of* Veal *White*.

Prepare your veal as above, and boil it, take a stew-pan with some good veal gravy, a few bread crumbs, let it boil to thicken a little, strain it thro' a sieve, put to it cream, a little mace, salt, oysters, mushrooms, and the sweet-bread cut in dices; lay your veal on the dish, and pour the ragoo hot upon it.

130. *To roll a* Breast *of* Veal.

Take a breast of veal, skin and bone it, lay it flat upon the table, and season it with mace and salt; make a stuffing of suet, bread crumbs, parsley shread, egg, pepper, salt and mace, beat in a mortar, and spread it all over the veal, roll it up and sew it, then tie it about with a string, and put a skewer through each end, lay it on a dish with butter over it, and put it into the oven; when its enough, cut it in three, and lay it on the dish. *For sauce*, gravy, butter, and sweet bread shread.

131. Veal *in Vale.*

Take the better end of a loin of veal, cut it into stakes, flat them with a clever, cover them with force-meat the thinkness of a crown, dip that side in egg which you lay your force-meat on; set a stew-pan over a stove with butter, put your veal in, a little fire over it till it be brown on both sides, then take them up, let the fat drain from them, and pour into the stew-pan some gravy, mushrooms, and truffles; so serve it up hot.

132. *To fry* Veal Sweet-Breads.

Take your sweet-breads and boil them in water, with a little salt and mace, let them stand till cold, then dip them in egg, dredge them with bread-crumbs, and fry them brown; serve them up with brown gravy, mushrooms, and truffles.

133. Veal Blanquet.

Roast a piece of veal, cut off the skin and nervous parts, cut it into thin slices; then put some butter into a stew-pan over the fire, with some shread onion, a little flour, put in the veal, and fry it a little, wet it with some good broth, and a little cream; season it with mace, salt, some young onions and parsley chopped small, and serve it up hot.

134. To stuff and roast a Fillet of Veal.

Mince beef suet very small, take bread-crumbs, sweet-herbs, egg, shread parsley, season them with pepper, salt, and nutmeg, beat in a mortar, cut holes and stuff the veal all over, spit it and put paper upon it to keep it from burning, and roast it; make your sauce of butter, gravy, and a little juice of lemon.

135. To make Veal Cutlets.

Take the best part of a loin of veal, cut it into stakes, flat them with a clever, rub them over with egg, and season them with mace and salt, dredge them with bread-crumbs, sweet-herbs, and parsley shread; lay them on a dripping pan, and set them before the fire, basting and turning them 'till they be brown on both sides; for sauce use butter, gravy and mushrooms.

136. To fry Calf's Feet.

Boil your calf's feet, and take out all the bones, lay them on a dish 'till they be cold;

mix

mix a little butter with eggs, flour and milk, not over thin, and have ready a stew-pan hot upon the fire with butter, in which dip the feet, and fry them brown; serve them up with butter in a boat, and currants plumped.

137. *To collar* CALF's FEET.

Boil them 'till tender, then take out all the bones, and season them with pepper, salt and mace, and sprinkle them over with shread parsley, lay them close together, tye them in a cloth, and bind them with a roller; boil them a quarter of an hour, then take them up, roll them tighter, and when cold put them in salt and water.

138. *To make* CALF's HEAD HASH.

After having cleaned your head, boil it, then take half of it, cut it in thin slices, and put it into a stew-pan, with some gravy, a little mace and salt, a glass of white wine, thicken it a little; then take the other half, and score it in squares, season it with pepper and salt, and rub it over with the yolk of an egg; and strew some crumbs of bread over it, and broil it; then take the brains, after being boiled, and mix with them an egg, a little flour and bread-crumbs, a little salt, pepper and nutmeg; fry them in little cakes and force-meat balls, and bacon; make your hash hot, and pour it on the dish; lay the broiled half in the middle, and the brain-cakes, balls, and bacon round.

139.

139. *To make* SHAM TURTLE.

Take a calf's head, clean and boil it, take out the bones, peel off the white skin, split the eyes and tongue; have ready some veal force-meat, wet it with egg, and season it with pepper, salt and mace, lay the force-meat upon a dish, and the tongue and eyes upon it; then lay the thick end to the small, and close together, laid it over the top with bacon, do it over with egg and bread-crumbs, and pour a pint of maderia on the dish, and set it in the oven; take a stew-pan, with brown gravy, a little chian pepper, morels and truffles; when the head is enough, lay it on the dish, skim off the fat, and pour the gravy into the stew-pan to the other gravy; make it hot and pour it on your dish.

140. *To make* SCOTS COLLOPS.

Take a fillet of veal, and cut it in thin slices, cut off the skins, and beat them with a paste pin, do them over with egg, and season them with mace and salt; set a stew-pan over a stove with a little butter, and when hot, dredge the collops with flour, and lay them in as many as will cover the bottom of the pan; have ready an earthen pot hot by the fire to put them in as you fry them; then put some good gravy into the stew-pan; put the collops on the dish with rashers of bacon and force meat balls; pour the gravy on hot.

140.

141. *To make* WHITE SCOTS COLLOPS.

Take a leg of veal, cut some thin slices, cut off the skins, and beat them with a paste-pin; season them with mace and salt, and fry them with butter, but not to be brown; put them in a pot to keep hot; then take some good veal gravy, cream, a little butter worked in flour, a little mace and salt, some mushrooms and oysters; boil some force meat balls, put the collops on the dish, and pour the sauce on hot.

142. *To make* FORCE-MEAT BALLS.

Take a pound of veal, and a pound and half of beef-suet clean from skin, chop them small, and beat them in a mortar; put in three eggs, a little mace, pepper, salt and nutmeg, work it up with bread-crumbs; if it be for brown, fry them; if for white, boil them. You may put the yolk of a boiled egg in some, and when you serve them, cut them in two.

143. *To make chopped* SCOTS COLLOPS.

Take part of a fillet of veal, free from skins, and shread it very fine, season it with salt and mace, make it up in cakes, and fry it in butter, lay them on your dish, and pour some hot gravy over them; serve them up with mushrooms and lemon.

144. *To make* VEAL OLIVES.

Cut some thin slices of a fillet of veal, season them with salt and mace; take a little of your veal and beat it fine with a little suet, bread-

bread-crumbs, two eggs, a little nutmeg and parsley; roll a piece of your forcemeat as big as an egg in every slice of your veal, sew them up, rub them over with egg and bread-crumbs; butter your dripping-pan, lay them on, and put them in the oven; when they are enough, serve them up with good gravy, morels and truffles.

145. *To make* VEAL ALLADABS.

Cut some slices of a leg of veal the thickness of your finger, make slits in them with the point of your knife, like the pockets of a hussif; then take some oysters, washed and shread, and fill the slits with them; do them over with egg, season them with mace and salt, and dredge bread-crumbs over them; fry them in butter, and serve them up hot, with good gravy, and sliced lemon.

146. *To make* BUMBAIS.

Cut some thin pieces of a fillet of veal in the form of a tart lid, and a sweet-bread in dices, some artichoke bottoms, marrow, and veal, and season them with mace and salt; lay them upon your veal, tuck them up close with skewers, and do them over with egg and bread-crumbs; brown them in a stew-pan with butter, take the skewers out, and lay them on your dish that side downwards; pour some good brown gravy on your dish, and serve them up hot.

147. *To make* PORK MITTOON.

Take a round pot, butter it, cut some

slices of slitched bacon, to cover the bottom of your pot and sides; then lay a layer of forcemeat, and a layer of thin slices of veal, seasoned with mace and salt, till the pot is filled; set it in the oven, and bake it, turning it on your dish the top downwards; pour on some good brown gravy and mushrooms.

148. *To make* PULLOW.

Take two chickens, singe and wash them, put them into a pot with veal or mutton, a little mace, three shallots, and a piece of bacon; take half a pound of rice, boil it in water till its enough, and drain it well; when your fowls are enough, send them up with some of the liquor they are stewed in, and the piece of bacon with them; then take your rice and cover them all over. You may stew sausages with them, if you please.

149. *To boil* CALF TONGUES.

Take four calf tongues, salt them with salt, bay-salt, and salt-petre; let them lay in pickle a week, then boil and blanch them; have ready a colliflower and some kidney-beans boiled, lay your tongues upon your dish, and your colliflower and kidney-beans betwixt them; they are a pretty dish cold, with butter, in the form of a pine-apple.

150. *To make* SHAM GOOSE.

Take a breast of pork, score it, cut a slit at each end to put your stuffing in; then take onion, sage and apple, shread small, sea-

season with pepper and salt; put the stuffing in, skewer it down, roast it, and sprinkle it with sage all over as it roasts; when its enough, serve it with gravy and apple sauce.

151. *To make* PORK GRISKINS.

Take a loin of pork, cut it in stakes, nick the skin, and flat them with the clever; season them with salt, pepper and sage, shread fine; set them before the fire to broil, turning them while they are enough; serve them with gravy and apple sauce.

152. *To roast a* LEG *of* PORK.

Take a leg of pork, salt it with common salt, let it lay five days, turn and rub the brine over it every day; then score the skin and roast it; put a little gravy on the dish, and serve it with apple sauce. If you chuse to boil one, let it lay ten days in the pickle.

153. *To salt a* HAM.

After your ham hath been kept twenty-four hours in a cool place, rub it well over with common salt, then take two ounces of salt-petre, one ounce of bay-salt beat fine, mixed with a handful of common salt; rub it well into the ham, and let it lay a fortnight, turning it every day, and rubbing in the brine; take it up to drain, dredge it with flour, and hang it to dry.

154. *To collar a* PIG'S HEAD.

Get the pig's head well cut off, clean it, and lay it in water twenty-four hours, changing the water till all the blood is sucked out; take it out of the water to drain, lay it with the bone side upwards; then take two ounces of salt-petre, and one ounce of bay-salt, beat them fine and sprinkle them upon the head; let it lay all night, then put it into a kettle of boiling spring water, and three neat's feet; let it boil till you can take the bones out; then lay the head on a cloth, the skin side downwards, laying the small part of one side, to the thick part of the other, lay the feet on, and salt it well; roll it up in the cloth, and tie it at each end; roll it up with a roller the breadth of your hand, put it into the kettle again, and let it boil an hour; then take it up, roll it tighter, and put it into an earthen pot with one end down, and a weight upon the other end; boil salt and water for the pickle; and when cold, take the head out of the cloth and put it into the pickle, making the pickle fresh every four or five days.

155. *To dress* Pig's Feet *and* Ears.

Boil pig's feet and ears tender, cut the ears long way, and split the feet in two, do them over with egg and bread-crumbs, and fry them; make the sauce of gravy, butter, mustard, and a little vinegar, put the ears in the sauce, make all hot, pour it on the dish, and lay on the feet.

156. *To roast a* Pig.

Put in the belly a piece of bread, some
sage

sage and parsley chopped small, and some salt; and sew it up; put a skewer thro' the fore and hind legs, and spit it; when warm, rub it all over with a feather dipped in oil, to prevent its blistering; when enough, cut the head off, then the ears, the under jaw, and chine it; take the brains, butter, gravy, sage and parsley boiled, make your sauce hot, pour it on your dish, and lay on your pig; plump some currants and send with it.

157. *To boil a* Pig.

Take a sucking pig, and boil it, when its enough, take the skin off, and cut it into quarters; use for sauce, butter, brains, sage and parsley; lay it on the dish with the head in the middle, and pour your sauce over it.

158. *To make* Pork Sausages.

Take three pounds of pork, fat and lean together, without skins or gristles, chop it very fine, season with pepper, salt, some sage shread fine, and egg; mix it well together; have the guts well cleaned, fill, and fry them.

159. *To make* Bolognia Sausages.

Take a pound of bacon, fat and lean together, a pound of beef suet, a pound of veal, a pound of pork, a pound of beef clear from skin and gristle, a handful of sage, and a few sweet herbs, chop them all small; and season well with pepper and salt. You must have

have a large gut, fill it, set on a pan with water, and when it boils, put it in; prick the gut for fear of bursting; boil it gently an hour, then lay it on clean straw to dry. They will keep good a year.

160. *To recover* VENISON *when its quick.*

Put it into boiling water half an hour, take it up and dry it with a cloth. It will do either for roasting or boiling.

161. *To roast a* HAUNCH *of* VENISON.

Take a haunch of venison, spit it, butter a paper, and lay over it, make a paste of brown meal and water, roll it into a sheet, and lay over it; then butter a paper and lay over the paste, tie it with pack-thread; half an hour before you draw it take off the paste and paper, and baste, dredge, and salt it. A haunch of twelve pounds weight, will take three hours roasting. Serve it with gravy and currant jelly.

162. *To roast a* NECK *of* VENISON.

Take off the skin, and skewer it on again, butter a paper, lay it on, and roast it; when its near enough take off the paper and skin, baste, dredge and salt it; serve it with gravy and currant jelly, or make a sauce of the pulps of apples, red wine, cinnamon and sugar.

163. *To fry* TRIPE.

Mix a batter of eggs, flour, and milk, dip in your tripes, and fry them crisp; peel and slice some onions, and fry them, lay the tripes

tripes on the dish, and the onions round; *for sauce*, use butter and mustard in a boat.

164. *To fricasy* Tripe *White*.

Take tripe, cut it into square pieces, and boil it tender; then take some veal gravy, a little cream, mace and salt; thicken it a little with butter rolled in flour, put in the tripes, and serve them hot.

165. *To roast a* Turkey.

Take your turkey, skewer the head to the side of the pinion, turn the feet upon the back, and break the breast-bone; make a forcemeat of bread-crumbs, a little suet, mace, salt, a few oysters, an egg, and stuff the breast, and roast it; when you serve it up, have gravy upon your dish, and bread sauce in a boat. *Make bread sauce thus*, Take a sauce pan with a little water, bread-crumbs, whole pepper, an onion, salt, and a little butter; boil them, then take out your onion and pepper, and pour it into your boat.

166. *To boil a* Turkey.

Take a turkey and truss it, take the breast bone out, cut the neck short, leave the skin long, singe it, and put it into milk and water; make a forcemeat, stuff the breast, tie the neck to keep in the forcemeat, put it in a cloth and boil it; *make your sauce* of melted butter, oysters, cream, a little mace, salt, and a few bread-crumbs, and pour it on hot.

167. *To make* Pulled Turkey.

Take a turkey, roast it, and when its enough, cut it up; take the white part, and cut it in long pieces, then put it into a saucepan, with a little thickened gravy, score and grill the legs; pour it upon your dish, and lay your legs upon it.

168. *To make* Turkey *A-la-daube.*

Truss a large turkey, break down the breast, and stuff the breast with some stuffing as you did the roast turkey, lard it with bacon; then rub the skin of the turkey over with the yolk of an egg, and strew over it a little mace, pepper, salt, and a few bread-crumbs; then put it into a copper-dish, and send it to the oven; when your dish is up make for it brown gravy sauce; shread into your sauce a few oysters and mushrooms, lay round artichoke bottoms fryed, stewed pallates, forcemeat-balls, and a little crisp bacon. Garnish your dish with pickled mushrooms and slices of lemon. This is proper for a remove.

169. *To roast* Turkey Pouts.

Take turkey pouts, cut the under jaw off, skewer their heads down to their legs, then stuff their breasts, and lard them with bacon; put their livers and gizzards in their pinions, and roast them; when you serve them up, put gravy on your dish, and bread sauce in a boat.

170. *To*

170. *To boil* Fowls.

Draw your fowls at the vent, cut the neck close off, leaving the skin to cover; break a little of the breast bone of the inside, put the legs in at the side of the belly, and skewer and singe them; put them in milk and water, and boil them. *For your sauce,* take a little veal gravy, bread-crumbs, a little cream, mace, a little melted butter, strain it thro' a sieve, and put in mushrooms; lay your fowls on a dish, and pour the sauce hot over them.

171. *To broil* Fowls.

Cut your fowls down the back, put in their legs, and flat them with a clever; season them with pepper, mace, and salt; take the pinions off, put a skewer in the legs to keep them from going together, and lay them before the fire to broil; baste, and dredge them with bread-crumbs. *For sauce,* gravy, butter, and a little lemon shread; serve them up hot with mushrooms.

172. *To roast* Fowls.

Take your fowls and singe them, take a little of the breast bone out of the inside, put the gizzards and livers in the pinions, cut the feet off, and roast them; when they are enough, put gravy on your dish, and parsley and butter in a boat.

173. *To roast* Capons.

Singe your capons, leave the heads on, scald the feet, take the skin and nails off, and turn the feet upon the backs; make a little stuffing for the breast, and roast them; when they are enough, put gravy on your dish. You may lard one, and leave the other unlarded.

174. *To boil* FOWLS *with* SELLERY.

Take your fowls and singe them, truss them for boiling, boil them white in milk and water, and a little salt; take some sellery, cut and wash it, boil it tender in salt and water, put your sellery into some melted butter with gravy; when they are enough, lay them on the dish, and pour your sauce hot over them.

175. PULLETS *roasted.*

Take them when they are full of eggs, draw and roast them, and when enough, cut them up and shread the brauny part in small slices, leaving the wings, legs and rumps whole; stew all in gravy with a little salt and mace, and a shread lemon, till enough; let the meat lay in the middle of the dish, with the legs, wings and rumps about it. Garnish with orange and lemon, quartered.

176. FOWLS *A-la-Praise.*

Take your fowls, draw and truss them, lard them with thick lards of bacon, season them with pepper, salt, mace and sweet-herbs; take a long deep stew-pan, and put in it some slices of bacon and veal; then put your fowls into it, moisten it with a glass of of white wine, and some gravy; stew it over your stove, turning your fowls till they are enough; make a ragoo of sweet-breads, veal-cockscombs, or oysters, which you like. Serve them up hot.

177. *To make* PULLETS SURPRIZE.

Roast them; if a small dish, one will be sufficient, take the lean of your pullet from the bone, cut it in thin slices an inch long, and tofs it up in a little cream, a little butter, with flour to make it the thickness of a good cream, put in a little pepper, salt, and mace; boil it up, and set it to cool; then cut six or seven thin round slices of bacon, put them in petty pans, lay some forcemeat on each slice, working them up on your hand, in the form and bigness of a French roll, with raw egg, leaving a hollow place in the middle; put in your fowls, and cover them with some of the same forcemeat, rubbing it smooth over with your hand and egg, throw some grated bread over them, and bake them in a gentle oven three quarters of an hour; let your sauce be made of butter and gravy, and a little thread lemon. Garnish with crisp parsley and orange.

178. *To hash* FOWLS.

Let your fowls be roasted, and cut them up; take a stew-pan, with a little gravy and butter rolled in flour, seasoned with a little pepper, and salt; make it hot, tho' if it boils it will make them hard; pour it upon your dish,

dish, and serve it up with bread fryed, and lemon.

179. *To boil* CHICKENS.

Dress your chickens neatly, finge, draw them at the vent, and trufs them; put a fkewer in the thick part of the leg, and one at the bottom, so that they may lay flat upon your difh; boil them in milk and water, and a little falt; for fauce, melted butter, a little creed rice, two fpoonfuls of white gravy, a little mace and falt; pour it over your chickens hot.

180. *To roaft* CHICKENS.

Pull your chickens dry, leave their heads on, draw and finge them, fcald their feet, and take their nails off; then put a fkewer thro' the thick part of the leg, take the head with it to the fide; fkewer the legs down to the vent, and roaft them; make the fauce of parfley and butter.

181. *To force* CHICKENS.

Raife the fkin on the breaft of your chickens with your fore-finger; take fome parfley, two anchovies fhread fmall, a little pepper, falt and nutmeg, work it up with butter, and ftuff your chicken breafts with it, lay a flice of bacon upon them, and roaft them; when your chickens are enough, take your bacon off, bafte and dredge them; for fauce, ufe parfley, anchovy, liver, and yolk of egg bruized fine; take a fauce-pan, with

a lita little gravy and melted butter, and put in your ingredients. Serve it up hot.

182. *To broil* CHICKENS.

Singe and truss your chickens, cut them down the backs, flat them with your clever, put a skewer in to keep them so, and lay the inside before the fire to broil; season them with a little mace and salt; baste and dredge them with bread-crumbs; and when they are enough, pour on your sauce made of gravy, butter and mushrooms

183. *To fry* CHICKENS.

Take four chickens, boil them almost enough, then cut them in pieces; take the juice of spinage, put it into the yolks of eight eggs, with some shread parsley and a grated nutmeg; your stew-pan being hot, with clarified butter, dip in your pieces of chickens in the green, batter and fry them gently on both sides; *for sauce*, melt your butter pretty thick, put in some juice of sorrel, a glass of white wine, make it hot, and pour it on your dish.

184. *To roast* DUCKS.

Take your ducks and singe them, scald and take their skins and nails off, their feet turn upon their backs, put a skewer through the thick part of their legs, and another through the bottom; rub the inside with a little pepper and salt, shread an onion, and some sage small, roll it up in a lump of butter, and put it into the belly; roast them,

and

and serve them with brown gravy on your dish.

185. *To boil* Ducks.

Take your ducks and skewer them as above, singe and put them into water, and boil them; for sauce, take six large onions, boil them till they are tender, changing the water several times, and chop them small; put a spoonful of cream to them to make them white; melt your butter, and put in your onions, with pepper and salt; make your sauce hot, lay your ducks on the dish, and pour it on.

186. *To make* Ducklings *A-la-mode.*

Take your ducklings, singe and bone them, season them with a little pepper and salt, and lay forcemeat in the inside of them; take a stew-pan with butter, put in your ducks and fry them; take them out and let them drain; then take a clean stew-pan with brown gravy, let them stew till they are enough, and serve them up.

187. *To roast a* Goose.

Take your goose, season it with pepper and salt, onion, sage, and an apple shread very small, work it with butter, and put it into the belly; put a skewer thro' the wings and the thick part of the legs, and another thro' the bottom part of the legs and the side bones; singe and roast it; and when enough, pour gravy upon your dish, and apple sauce upon a plate.

188. *To*

188. *To boil a* Goose.

Singe and skewer your goose, wash it well in water, and boil it in salt and water; cut the white part of sellery half an inch long, wash and boil it in salt and water, till its tender; and pour it into a sieve, to drain; melt some butter and put in your sellery, lay your goose on a dish, and pour your sauce hot over it.

189. *To dry a* Goose.

Take a fat goose, and dress it; then a quarter of a pound of common salt, an ounce of saltpetre, an ounce of bay-salt, beat and mix them all together, rub your goose very well inside and out, with it; let it lay a week, turning and rubbing it every day with the brine; then hang it up to dry; when well dried, lay it in a dry place, and you may keep it two or three months; when you boil it, let it have a good deal of water. You may have turnips or cabbage, boiled and stewed, or onion sauce.

190. *To make* Geese *A-la-Mode.*

Take two geese, raise their skins on the breast, and make a stuffing of sweet-breads, mushrooms, anchovies, oysters and marrow; a little pepper, salt, nutmeg and thyme, mix all these together with the yolk of egg; put a little under the skin on the breast, and some in the bellies; lard your geese with lemon peel, then brown them, and put them in strong gravy, seasoned very high; when they are stewed enough, take them out, put

in

in a gill of claret and thicken it a little; make it hot, lay your geese on the dish, and pour your sauce over 'em.

191. *To roast a* Green Goose.

Rub your goose in the inside with a little salt, put a lump of butter in it, skewer and roast it; when it is enough, put gravy on your dish, and butter, juice of sorrel, and gooseberries, in a boat.

192. *To stew* Geese Giblets.

Scald and pick them clean, break the two pinion-bones; cleave the head; cut off the nostrils; take the eyes out; slip the skin off the neck; cut them in three, and the liver in two; take the skin off the gizzard and slice it, break the feet and take the nails off; wash and put them into a stew-pan, with a quart of good mutton broth, a bundle of sweet herbs, an onion, some whole pepper, and a blade of mace; cover them close, and let them stew till quite tender; then take a french roll, toast it brown on all sides, and put it into the stew-pan, giving it a shake, let it stew till there is just gravy enough to eat them with; take out the spice and herbs, put the roll on the middle of the dish and your giblets round, and pour on your sauce.

193. *To roast* Pigeons.

Fill them with parsley clean wash'd and chopped, and pepper and salt rolled in butter; tye the neck close, put a skewer thro' the the legs, and roast them; when they are enough,

enough, pour parsley and butter, on your dish.

194. *To boil* Pigeons.

Take your pigeons, put the legs into the sides, wash and boil them; then serve them up with stewed spinnage and grilled bacon; for sauce have parsley and butter in a boat.

195. *To make a* Palpatoon *of* Pigeons.

Take savoury force-meat, rolled out like paste, put it in a butter'd dish, lay a layer of thin bacon, season your pigeons, and lay them in; slice a sweet-bread, asparagus-tops, mushrooms, cockscombs, and the yolks of hard eggs; make of them another forcemeat and lay it over them, bake them, and when enough, turn them into a dish, and pour gravy into it.

196. *To broil* Pigeons *whole*.

Take your pigeons, singe them, and put the legs in at the sides, make a stuffing of shread parsley, hard yolks of eggs, bread-crumbs, pepper, salt, and mace, work it up with butter, put a little into the bellies, rub them over with egg and bread-crumbs, lay them on a dish, and set them into the oven; when they are enough, put gravy and butter upon your dish.

197. Pigeons *transmogrified*.

Take your pigeons, season them with pepper and salt, roll a piece of puff paste, and wrap round each pigeon, put them in a cloth and tie them so that your paste do not break;

break; boil them an hour in a good deal of water; loose them carefully, least they should break; lay them on your dish, and pour on a little gravy. You may do them the same way and bake them.

198. PIGEONS *in a Hole*.

Take your pigeons, singe and season them, put a bit of butter in their bellies; butter a dish and lay them in; make batter of milk, eggs, and flour, which pour all over them; bake them, and send them to the table.

199. *To jug* PIGEONS.

Pull and draw your pigeons, and singe them, but do not wash them; take the livers, give them a scald in water, and bruise them with the yolks of two hard eggs, some lemon peel and parsley shread fine, suet and breadcrumbs, pepper, salt, and nutmeg; work them up with raw egg, and put a piece into the crops and bellies; sew up the neck and vent, dip them in water, and season them with white pepper and salt; put them in a jug, and set them in a kettle of cold water, cover the jug close up, and let it boil three hours; then take them out of the jug, and lay them in the dish; thicken your gravy a little, and pour it on your pigeons.

200. *To grill* PIGEONS.

Take your pigeons, singe and put their legs in their sides, cut them down their backs, and flat them with your clever; put a skewer in to keep them flat, then lay them upon

upon the grid-iron, over a flow fire, not to make them black; throw a little pepper and salt on the inside, and turn them; when they are enough, put a little hot gravy upon your dish; take a little butter upon the point of a knife, rub them over, and lay them on your dish.

201. PIGEONS *stoved*.

Take a small cabbage lettice, just cut out the heart, make a force-meat, and chop the heart of the cabbage with it; then fill up the hole, and tie it across with a pack-thread, and fry it a light brown, in fresh butter; pour out all the fat, lay the pigeons round, flat them with your hand, and season them a little with pepper, salt, and beaten mace; take care not to put in too much salt; pour in half a pint of white wine, cover it close, and let it stew five or six minutes; then put in a gill of good gravy, cover them close, and let them stew half an hour; take a good piece of butter rolled in flour, and shake it in; when its thick, take it up, untie it, lay the lettice in the middle, and the pigeons round; put in a little lemon juice, and pour the sauce over them; stew a little lettice, and cut it in pieces. Garnish with red pickled cabbage.

202. PIGEONS *in* SURTOUT.

Stuff your pigeons; then lay a slice of bacon on each breast, and a slice of veal beat with the back of a knife, season'd with mace,

pep-

pepper, and salt, tye them on, then spit your pigeons on a small spit, and roast them; baste 'em first with butter, then with the yolk of an egg, dredge them with bread-crumbs, a little nutmeg, and sweet herbs; when enough lay them in your dish, and have ready good gravy, with truffles, morels, and mushrooms, to pour into your dish. Garnish with lemon.

203. *To pickle* PIGEONS.

Take your pigeons and bone them, beginning at the neck, and turning the skin down; when they are boned, season them with nutmeg, pepper, and salt, sew up both ends, and boil them in water, white wine, vinegar, salt, and whole pepper; when they are enough, take them out of the pickle, and boil it with a little more salt; when it is cold, put in your pigeons, and keep them for use.

204. *To roast* PARTRIDGES.

Draw and truss your partridges, and roast them; when you serve them up have browned crumbs of bread on your dish, and brown gravy and bread sauce in your boats.

205. *To boil* PARTRIDGES.

Draw, singe, and truss your partridges, take off their feet, and boil them; for sauce, take some sellery and cut it half an inch long, boil it in salt and water till tender, and drain it; melt some butter and put in your sellery, lay your partridges on the dish, and pour on your sauce.

206. YOUNG PARTRIDGES *with* OYSTERS.

Pick some young partridges, draw and singe them, mince oysters, a little parsley, a little pepper and salt, work it up with a little butter, and put it into their bellies; spit them, cut a slice of bacon, and wrap round them; when they are enough, take off the bacon, baste, and dredge them; take some brown gravy and oysters, made hot, and pour it on your partridges on the dish. Do not roast them too much.

207. *A Hash of* PARTRIDGES.

After having roasted your partridges, cut them up; take a stew-pan with gravy, a shallot shread to a pulp, put in your partridges. You may thicken it a little, and season it to your taste; cover it, and set it on your stove, but not to boil. When it is hot serve it up.

208. *To roast a* PHEASANT.

Pick and draw your pheasant, leaving the head and feet on, skewer and roast it; and when its enough, serve it with brown gravy on your dish; gild the bill, tie the tail-feathers together, and tuck them in the vent; have bread sauce in a boat.

209. *To boil a* PHEASANT.

Pick, draw, and skewer your pheasant, stump the legs, and leave the head on, boil it in a good deal of water; boil some sellery tender, put it into a little melted butter, with a little salt to your taste; lay your phea-

pheasant on the dish, and pour your sauce over it.

210. *To stew a* Pheasant

Stew it in veal gravy; take artichoke bottoms parboiled, and some chesnuts blanched; when your pheasant is enough, skim the gravy, put in the chesnuts and artichoke bottoms, with a little mace beat, pepper and salt to season it, and a glass of white wine; and if you do not think it thick enough, put in a bit of butter rolled in flour; put in a little juice of lemon, pour the sauce over the pheasant, and have some forcemeat balls fryed to put into the dish.

211. *To boil a* Peacock.

Flea off the skin, but leave the rump whole, with the pinions; then mince the flesh raw, with some beef suet, season'd with salt, pepper, nutmeg, and some sweet-herbs shread small, mix them all together with egg, and fill the skin of your peacock; sew it in the back, and set it to stew in a deep dish, in some strong broth, white wine, a little salt, mace, marrow, artichokes boiled and quartered, chesnuts, grapes, barberries, pears quartered, and some of the meat made in balls; cover it with another large dish, and when its stewed enough, serve it up with sippets. Garnish with sliced lemon, and lemon peel whole, run it over with melted butter, and the yolks of hard eggs and chesnuts.

212. *To roast* Moor-Game.

Pick and draw them, leave the head and feet on, skewer them as a pheasant, and singe and roast them; when they are enough, pour gravy on your dish, and bread sauce in a boat.

213. *To roast a* Guiney-Hen.

Pick, draw, and singe it, skewer it as you do moor game, lard it with bacon, and roast it; put gravy on the dish, and bread sauce in a boat.

214. *To roast* Wild Ducks.

Pick, draw, and skewer them, with their feet upon the backs, and their stumps upward, cut the neck off close, leaving the skin, and put a bit of salt and butter in the belly, singe and roast them; for sauce, use a little brown gravy, and red wine on your dish.

215. *To dress a* Wild Duck.

Half roast your duck, then take it off the spit, and lay it on a dish; carve it, but leave the joints hanging together in all the incisions, put on salt, pepper, and the juice of lemon or orange; turn it on the breast; press it hard with a plate, put to it a little gravy, and set it to stew, turning it; serve it up hot in its own gravy.

216. *To dress a* Ruddock.

It is a water bird, much like a duck, but the flesh is more delicious than that of ducks; dress it in the same manner you do ducks.

217. *To roast a* Wild-Goose.

Take a wild goose and skewer it as you do a tame goose, put a bit of pepper and salt in the belly, singe and roast it; for sauce, use gravy and red wine upon the dish.

218. Ortolans *roasted.*

Bard them, or let them be plain, putting a vine leaf betwixt them; when they are spitted, some crumbs of bread may be used as for larks; its the best to spit them side-ways.

219. Ortolans *fryed.*

After they are fryed, soak them in a little broth, put them in a stew-pan with butter, and season them well; to thicken the sauce, mix with it some sweet breads shread, a little gravy and mushrooms; and when all is well stewed, serve it up. Garnish with pistachos and pomegranate.

220. *To dress* Ruffs *and* Reifs.

They are Lincolnshire birds, and you may fatten them with white-bread, milk and sugar; they feed fast, and will die in their fat, if not killed in time; pick and draw them, turn their feet upon their backs, and spit them side-ways; roast them with vine leaves upon them, and when they are near enough, take off the leaves, and serve them quick with gravy and butter.

221. *To roast* Wood-Cocks.

Pick them, turn their feet upon their backs, cut their wings off as you do a duck, put a skewer through the thighs and the head, for the legs and bill to stand up, spit them side-ways, and have ready a toast of bread to set under for the train to drop on; then lay your toasts on the dish, pour on butter with a little gravy, and lay on your woodcocks.

222. *To roast* SNIPES.

You must roast them the same way as you do woodcocks, with toasts.

223. *To roast* THRUSHES.

Pick them clean, truss them, put them upon a skewer, tie them to a spit, and roast them, basting and dredging them with crumbs of bread; take a little gravy and a shallot shread small; when they are enough, make your gravy hot, and pour it on your dish, and lay on your birds. You may roast lap-wings after the same manner.

224. *To roast* QUAILS.

Truss your quails, put into their bellies a little butter and salt, and a few sweet herbs shread; put them on a small spit to roast, and when they are warm, baste them with salt and water, a little at the first; then dredge and baste them with butter; take a little gravy, shread an anchovy, and put into it, with two or three shallots, sliced and boiled, make it hot and serve them up.

225. *To roast* WOODCOCKS *the French Way*.

Get some wood cocks, pull, draw, wash, and truss them; then lard them with bacon,

D and

and roast them; serve them upon toasts dipped in the juice of orange, with the gravy made warm.

226. *To roast* PLOVER.

Take your plover, pick and draw them, cut the necks off close, turn their feet back, put a skewer thro' their thighs, and roast them; serve them up with gravy and butter on your dish.

227. *To roast* TEAL.

Take your teal, pick and draw them, cut their necks off close, skewer them as you do a wild duck, grate a little nutmeg and salt, which put into them, and roast them; serve them up with gravy and red wine upon your dish.

228. PLOVERS CAPUCINE.

Take four hog's ears, boil them tender, put a piece of force-meat and your birds in the ears, with the heads outwards, set them upright, the tips of the ears falling backwards; wash them with eggs and crumbs, then bake them gently; and serve them up with gravy.

229. *To boil* TEAL.

Dress your teal and skewer them, take oysters, a few sweet-herbs, parsley and sage, shred them, work them up with a little butter and pepper, and put into their bellies; tie their necks and vents, and when your water boils put in the teal, boil them tender, and serve them up with gravy, anchovy sauce, and oysters.

230. *To roast* TEAL *with* OLIVES.

Mince the livers with parsley, onions, mushrooms, scraped bacon, and a bit of butter, mix altogether, and put them into the bellies of your teal; then wrap them up in slices of bacon, paper and roast them; while they are roasting, take out the stones of your olives, blanch them, put them in a stew-pan with a little veal gravy, and let them have a boil; your teal being ready, take off the paper and bacon, and dish them up with your ragoo of olives over them.

231. *To boil* RAIES.

Cut off their heads and legs, truss them, and put them into a stew-pan with strong broth, and a gill of white wine; season them with salt, pepper, whole mace, and currants; when they are enough, dish them on sippets; thicken your broth with bread-crumbs and butter, a little juice of lemon, and serve them up hot.

232. *To stew* LAPWINGS.

Pick, draw, and singe them, cut them in two, put them in a stew-pan, with an onion cut small, some butter, a veal sweet-bread shread, give them a fry, and put to them gravy, a little white wine, and mushrooms; let them simmer, 'till they are enough, skim off the top, let them be well tasted, and serve them up hot.

233. *To roast a* Hern.

Let the hern be picked, lard the breast and back, roast, and baste it with butter and white wine, dredge it with sweet-herbs shread, and bread-crumbs; make a sauce of the yolks of eggs beaten, anchovies, a little claret and vinegar; when its roasted, serve it up. Garnish with lemon and orange.

234. *To stew a* Heath Cock.

Flea off the skin, leave the rump, legs and pinions whole, mince the flesh with beef suet, seasoned with salt, pepper, and sweet-herbs minced, and raw yolks of eggs; mix these all well together, with three artichoke bottoms boiled, blanched chesnuts, marrow, skirrets boiled and minced small; then fill the skin, and prick it up, stew it in a deep stew-pan with strong broth, marrow, mace, white wine, salt, artichokes quartered, chesnuts, barberries, grapes, and pears quartered, and some of the minced meat made into balls; when its done, serve it up with sippets, and yolks of hard eggs.

235. *To roast* Dotterels.

Take dotterels, pick, draw, and truss them, singe and wrap them about with a slice of bacon, spit them, and lay them down to roast; when they are near enough, take off your bacon, baste and dredge them, and serve them up with gravy and butter on your dish.

236. *To roast* LARKS.

Pick them, and cut off their necks close, turn their feet back, put them on a skewer, and tie them on a spit, singe and baste them, dredge them with crumbs of bread; then break some eggs at the end, pour the egg out, and wash the shells; when they are dry, put some dryed crumbs of bread, and a roasted lark in every shell, have crumbs upon your dish, and serve them up as eggs in shells.

237. *To dress* LARKS *Pear Fashion*.

Pick them, and cut their necks close and their legs off; season them with salt, pepper, and mace; make a forced-meat, and wrap up every lark in the shape of a pear; stick one leg in the top, like the stalk of a pear, rub them over with the yolk of an egg and bread-crumbs; bake them in a gentle oven; so serve them up, You may garnish any other birds with them.

238. *To roast a* HARE.

Case your hare, cut off the feet, wash it, and put the wings into the breast, give a cut on each side the tail to let the legs fall to the side; take a skewer and put it thro' the legs and cheek for it to lay round; take some bread-crumbs, suet, mace, pepper and salt, and a few sweet-herbs, wet them with egg, and beat them in a mortar, roll it up, put it into the belly, and sew it up; tie the legs with a string, to keep them from starting; spit it and lay it down to roast; if it is an old

old one, baste it a little at the first with milk, for to tender it; afterwards you may baste it with butter; when it is enough, pour gravy and butter on your dish; have sweet sauce in a boat, made of pulp of apple, red wine, sugar, and cinnamon, or currant jelly. You may gild the ears, or you may lard it, if you please.

239. *To roast a* LEVERET.

Case it, but leave its ears and feet on, put a skewer down the neck for the head to stand up, also another thro' its hind legs, and another thro' its fore-feet and breast, for to lay flat; lay it down to roast, and baste it with butter; when its enough, pour gravy on your dish, and have sweet sauce in a boat. Gild the ears.

240. *To roast a* HARE *with the Skin on.*

Take out the bowels, wipe the inside with a clean cloth, make a pudding as in the former receipt, put it into the belly, and sew it up; thrust your hand between the skin and the body, and rub butter and spice incorporated together, over the flesh, then sew up the hole of the skin and roast it, basting it with boiling water and salt, till its above half roasted; then let it dry, till the skin smoke, and pull it off by pieces; then baste it with butter, and dredge it with flour, grated bread and spice; make a sauce of butter, gravy, and claret.

241. *To fry a* HARE.

Case it, cut off the wings and legs whole, and

and cut the reſt in pieces; take a ſtew-pan with butter, dredge your hare, and lay it in, and when fryed on one ſide, ſlice ſome onions, put them into your ſtew-pan, with a little mace, pepper and ſalt, gravy, and red wine, as much as will do for ſauce; let it ſimmer, and ſerve it up hot.

242. *To make* CIVET *of a* HARE.

Take out all the bones and ſinews of the hair, cut one half in thin ſlices, and the other half in pieces an inch thick, flour them, and fry them in butter quick as collops; have ready ſome gravy, made good with the bones of the hare and beef, put a pint of it into the pan to the hare, ſome muſtard, and a little elder vinegar, cover it cloſe, and let it boil ſoftly 'till its as thick as cream; then diſh it up with the head in the middle.

243. *To dreſs a* HARE *the Swiſs Way.*

Cut the hare in quarters, lard it, put it into a ſtew-pan, with good broth, and a little wine, ſeaſon'd with ſalt, pepper, and cloves; while it is ſtewing, toſs up the blood and liver ſhred, with a little flour in a ſtew-pan, put in ſome capers, ſton'd olives, and a drop of vinegar, and ſerve it up.

244. *A jugged* HARE.

Cut it into handſome pieces, lard it with little ſlips of bacon, ſeaſon it with pepper, ſalt, and mace, lay it into a jug, put half a pound of butter over it, and tie it cloſe; either ſend it to the oven, or put it in a pot of boiling water three hours; when its enough, put it into the stew-pan, skim off the top, and put the gravy to the hare with a little more good gravy to it; thicken it a little, make your hare hot in it, and serve it up.

245. *To roast* Rabbets.

Take a couple of rabbets, case and skewer them side to side; while they are roasting, boil some parsley and the livers shread very small, and mix'd with melted butter; when they are enough, cut off their heads, and cleave them in two; pour your sauce upon the dish, lay on your rabbets, and the heads on each side. You may put a pudding in their bellies, if you chuse.

246. *To boil* Rabbets.

Case and truss them as you do a hare for roasting, put them in milk and water, and boil them; boil some onions tender, changing the water, shread them small, and mix them with melted butter, a little cream, a little pepper and salt, and when the rabbets are boil'd enough, pour it over them.

247. *To dress* Rabbets *Moorgame Way.*

Take young rabbets and case them, cut off their wings and heads, bone them half way, pull off the skins, but leave the feet and claws on, put in a little forc'd-meat, double your rabbets up, and skewer them like a fowl; put a skewer at the bottom thro' the legs and neck, and tie it with a string

string to prevent them from flying open; put gravy on your dish, and bread sauce in a boat.

248. *To dress* RABBETS *with* BACON.

You must case them and leave the heads on; take out all the bones, season them with a little mace and salt, lay thin slices of bacon upon them, roll them up tight; turn the heads and skewer them to the side, tie each end with a string to keep it close; you must lay them on a dish to bake, put butter over them, and dredge them; *for sauce*, use parsley, liver and butter.—Three will be enough for a dish; lay them with their heads in the middle.

249. *To make* PULLED RABBETS.

Take two young rabbets, and boil them in milk and water, pull the meat in shives and put it into your stew-pan, with a little white gravy, a glass of white wine, a little salt and nutmeg, thicken it a little; and when you serve it up, lay the heads in the middle. Garnish with sliced lemon.

250. *To stew* RABBETS *the French Way*.

Divide your rabbets into quarters, lard them with pretty large lardoons of bacon, and fry them; stew them in a stew-pan with strong broth, white wine, salt, pepper, a faggot of sweet herbs fryed, flour and orange.

251. *A* FRICASEY *of* RABBETS.

Case your rabbets, and cut them in quarters, flour and fry them brown in butter, put some gravy into a stew-pan with mushrooms, morels, artichoke bottoms, and put in your rabbets seasoned to your taste; set it over the fire, and make it hot, tho' not to boil; dish your rabbets, and pour your sauce over them.

252. *A White* Fricasy *of* Rabbets.

Take two young rabbets, half boil them, and cut them up; take a stew-pan, with some white gravy, and crumbs of bread; when they are steeped a little, press them thro' a sieve; to thicken your gravy, put the rabbets into your stew-pan with a little cream, oysters, mushrooms, a little mace, salt, nutmeg, and butter; set it over your stove to be hot, tho' not to boil; serve it up with your sauce as thick as good cream.

253. *To* Fricasy Chickens.

Take two or more chickens, and half roast them, cut them up as you would do for eating, skin them, take off half the pinion and the ends of the bones, to make them look well; take a stew-pan with some white gravy, thicken it with bread, and strain your gravy thro' a sieve; put it into your stew-pan with the chickens, a little mace, nutmeg, salt, and butter, roll'd in flour, a little cream, and mushrooms; set it over your stove to simmer, and when you serve it up, leave out the neck part.

254. *A brown* Fricasy *of* Chickens.

Take your chickens, singe and cut them up, flat them a little, and fry them brown; put

put them in your stew-pan with a little gravy, and white wine, season'd to your taste; thicken it a little, and serve it up hot.

255. *To fricasy* SWEET-BREADS.

Take your sweet-breads, and boil them in water, salt, whole pepper, and mace; when they are enough, lay them on your dish, and have ready a white sauce made like your fricasy, to pour over them.

256. *A* FRICASY *of* PIGS *Feet and Ears.*

Take four pig's feet and four ears, boil them tender, cut the ears long, and split the feet, take out the great bones, then put them into a stew-pan, with some white gravy, a little cream, mace, salt, butter and bread-crumbs; strain it thro' a sieve, and serve it up hot.

257. *A* FRICASY *of brown* TRIPES.

Take your tripes, boil them tender, and cut them long; have some good brown gravy thicken'd, give them a shake, and serve them up hot.

258. *A* FRICASEY *of* EGGS.

Boil eight eggs hard, and cut them in quarters; take a little brown gravy, salt, mace, white wine, and thicken it; lay your eggs on the dish, and pour your sauce hot over them.

259. *A White* FRICASY *of* EGGS.

Boil your eggs hard, cut some in quarters, and have some whole yolks; make a white sauce as you do for other fricasys,

and

and pour it over them; cut three of the hard yolks, and lay round them.

260. *A* Fricasy *of* Mushrooms.

Rub your small mushrooms, peel the large ones, and cut them in four; put them first in water, then take them out and put them in a pan over the fire to stew gently; put in a little salt, and when they are enough, take them out of the liquor to drain; then put them into a stew-pan, with a little cream and some of their own liquor, a piece of butter rolled in flour, a little mace and whole pepper; make them hot, take out the pepper, and serve them up.

261. *To* Fricasy Artichoke Bottoms.

Scrape the bottoms clean, boil them, and cut them in large dices, put them in a little white gravy and cream, and a little butter rolled in flour; season them with salt, pepper and nutmeg, give them a shake over the fire, and serve them up hot.

262. *To* Fricasy *a* Pig.

Half roast your pig, then take it up, and strip off the coat; pull the meat in flakes from the bones, and put it into a stew-pan with some gravy, white wine, a little vinegar, an onion stuck with cloves, some mace, a bunch of sweet herbs, some salt and lemon-peel; when its almost enough, take out the onion, herbs and lemon-peel, and put in some mushrooms; thicken it with cream. The head must be roasted whole and set in the middle

middle of the dish, and the fricasy round it. Garnish with sliced lemon.

263. *To* Fricasey Skirrets.

Wash the roots very well, and boil them 'till they are tender; then take off the skins, and cut the roots in slices; have ready a little cream, a piece of butter rolled in flour, the yolk of an egg beat, a little white wine and nutmeg grated, and salt, mix all together, and pour the sauce over the roots in your dish.

264. Eggs *with* Endive.

Blanch some endive, press it well, give it two or three cuts with a knife, and put it into a stew-pan, wet it with a little gravy, and let it stew half an hour; poach half a dozen eggs, and trim them; pour the endive on your dish, lay your eggs in order upon it, and serve it up hot.

265. *To make* Stuffed Eggs.

Take a dozen eggs and boil them hard, peel and cut them in two, take the yolks out of them, and put them in a mortar, with a piece of butter, some young onions, parsley and mushrooms shread, a little bread steeped in cream, season and pound them all together; then fill the whites of your eggs with it, and smooth them with a knife and raw egg; put some stuffing in the dish you intend to serve them in, set your eggs in order, and bake them in an oven; when they are enough, pour on them a little hot gravy.

266. *To make* Eggs *in* Moonshine.

Break your eggs into a dish upon some oil either melted or cold, strew some salt on them, and set them over a chaffing-dish of coals, and cover them; but make not the yolks too hard; make your sauce of an onion cut in round slices, and fried in good oil; put to them a little verjuice, salt and grated nutmeg, and serve them up hot.

267. Eggs *with the* Juice of Sorrel.

Poach your eggs, pound some sorrel, and put the juice of it into a dish, with some butter, two or three raw eggs, and some salt and nutmeg; make all this into a sauce, and pour it on your poached eggs, so serve them up.

268. Eggs *with* Anchovies.

Poach your eggs, lay them in a dish, and trim them round with a knife; then melt some butter, with anchovies, fry'd flour, salt and juice of lemon; pour it upon them, and serve them up.

269. *To make an* Amblet of Eggs.

Take what quantity of eggs you want, beat them well, and season them with salt and whole pepper, to your liking; have ready your frying-pan with a good deal of fresh butter made hot; put in your eggs with four spoonfuls of strong gravy; have cut parsley and cives to throw over them, turning them 'till enough; squeeze the juice of a lemon or orange over them, and serve them for a side-dish.

270. *To*

270. EGGS *with* SPINAGE.

Boil your spinage, and squeeze it dry; take a stew-pan with a little gravy and butter, put in your spinage to stew a little; poach six eggs, fry some sippets, to lay round your spinage, and put the eggs upon it.

271. *To make an* EGG *as large as six.*

Take six eggs, part the yolks from the whites, and boil them in a bladder 'till they are hard; then take them out, put them into another bladder, and pour the whites round; tie them up oval or round, and boil them. You may serve them with sallads.

272. *To make* BUBBLE *and* SQUEAK.

Take cabbage, boil and drain it, cut it small, and put it into a stew-pan with butter, and some young onions cut small; take some slices of beef that hath been either boiled or roasted, fry them, and put to them a little vinegar, pepper, salt, and a spoonful of gravy. Serve it up hot.

273. *To pot* LOBSTERS.

Take your lobsters, boil them, take out the meat of the tail and claws, and season them with salt, mace and pepper; put them into a pot, lay butter over them and bake them; when they come out of the oven, take them out of the pot, put them into long pots, and clear off the butter that they were baked in, and add a little fresh butter; bruise the seed of your lobsters, and put it into the butter, make it hot and pour it into your pots, and set them to cool for use.

274. *To pot* BEEF.

Take as much beef as you think proper, cut it in pieces, take some salt-petre and common-salt, and season it, put it into a pot, lay half a pound of butter over it, and let it stand all night in the oven to stew; take the beef with gravy and butter into a mortar, and beat them fine; if its not seasoned enough, put more to it; put it close down in long pots, and when cold cover them over with butter, and keep them for use.

275. *To pot* VENISON.

Take your venison, cut it in pieces, season it with salt, mace and pepper, and a little salt-petre; put it into a pot with some butter over it, and set it in the oven all night; when its baked, beat it in a mortar, take off the fat, with a little of the gravy; when you have beat it, put it into your pots, pressed down, and when cold, cover it with butter, and keep it for use.

276. POTTED HARE.

Wash your hare clean, wipe it with a cloth from the blood, cut it in pieces, and season it with salt, mace, pepper and nutmeg, put it into a pot, lay a pound of butter over it, let it stand in the oven all night; then take the bones out and beat the meat in a mortar; skim off the top and beat with it, put it into your

pots,

pots, prefs it down, and cover it over with butter.

277. POTTED PORK.

Take a flefhy piece of pork, fkin it, cut it in pieces, and beat it in a mortar with fage, pepper and falt; put it in a pot, lay a little butter over it, and bake it; when it comes out of the oven, take it out with care, and drain it from the gravy; put it in a dry pot preffed clofe down, fkim off all the top of the gravy, put butter to it, and pour it over your pots.

278. *To pot* SALMON *as at Newcaftle.*

Scale your falmon, and wipe it very clean, but do not wafh it; take out the bone, then cut it the fhape of your pot; feafon it with falt, mace, cloves and whole pepper, lay four bay leaves on it, and cover it over with butter; bake it, and when it is enough, take it out to drain from the gravy; then put it into the pot to keep, and when cold, cover it over with butter.

279. *To pot* CHARRS.

After having cleaned them, cut off the fins, tails, and heads, lay them in rows in a long baking pot, feafoned with falt, pepper and mace, and put butter over them; to four pounds of charrs, put two pounds of butter; when they are baked, take them out of the pot to drain, pour a little butter into the pot you intend to keep them in, lay in the fish pressed down, skim off the butter from the gravy, and pour it over them.

280. *To pot* RABBETS.

Case and wipe them clean, cut them in pieces, and lard them; season them with salt, pepper, mace and nutmeg, lay them in your pot, put butter over them, and bake them; when they are enough, take the bones out, beat the meat in a mortar, with a little of the top skimmed off the gravy, 'till fine, fill your pots pressed down hard, and pour butter over them.

281. *To pot* MUSHROOMS.

Rub small mushrooms with a woollen-cloth, those that will not rub, peel and take out the gills, and put them into water as you do them; when they are all done, wipe them dry, put them in a sauce-pan, with a handful of salt, and a piece of butter; stew them till they are enough, shaking them often, for fear of burning, drain them from their liquor, and when they are cold wipe them dry; lay them in a pot one by one, as close as you can, 'till it be full, clarify some butter, and let it stand 'till almost cold, then pour it into your mushrooms; when cold, cover them with butter and flour close in your pot; and when you use them, wipe them clean from the butter, stew them in gravy thickened as when fresh.

282. *To pot* TROUTS.

Scale and clean your trouts very well, wash

wash them in vinegar, cut them down the backs, and season them very well with pepper and salt; lay them in a pot with butter over them, and bake them; when they are enough, take them out of your pot to drain, and lay them into a long pot, and when cold, pour butter over them.

283. *To make* POTTED VEAL.

Take part of a fillet of veal, cut it in lumps, and season it with mace, pepper and salt, put it into a pot, lay butter over it and bake it; when it is enough, beat it in a mortar, moistened with a little of the gravy, when it is beat fine, put it into your pots, pressed hard down, and when cold, pour butter over it.

284. *To pot* MOOR-GAME.

Pick, draw, and wipe them clean, cut off their heads, and season them with mace, pepper, and salt; lay them close in a pot with the feet in the middle, with butter over them; bake them 'till they are enough, then drain the gravy from them, and when cold, pour butter over them. You may pot partridges, larks, pigeons, pheasants, or any other birds the same way.

285. *To pot* WOODCOCKS.

Pick them, and take that bit out of the top of the neck which makes them eat bitter if left in, but do not draw them; season them very well with mace, pepper and salt, lay them close in the pot with their bills in

the

the middle, and butter over them; bake them 'till they are enough; set them to cool, and when cold, pour butter over them. In seasoning any thing for potting, put in white pepper, for it makes them look cleaner; in all potted things, take care to clarify your butter before you pour it on, and if you turn your pots up side down, they will keep much longer in a cool place.

286. *To make* PASTE *for a* PASTY.

Take six pounds of flour, and four pounds of butter, put a pound in small pieces into your flour; break four eggs into some cold water and work them into paste; then roll it out thin, put more butter over it, and dredge it over with flour, roll it up in three times rolling out, you may put all your butter in, dredging it every time you roll it out; make it in a cool place, and handle it as little as you can.

287. *To make* PASTE *for a* GOOSE PYE.

Take six pounds of butter, and boil it in a gallon of water, skim it off, into a peck of flour, and as little of the liquor as you can, work it up into a paste; then pull it into pieces 'till cold, and make it up into what form you please.

288. *To make* PASTE *for* TARTS.

Take a pound of flour, and half a pound of butter, rub the butter into the flour, two eggs, and a little water, and make it into a paste.

289. *To*

289. *To make* SHELL PASTE.

Take half a pound of flour, a quarter of a pound of butter, an egg, two ounces of sugar sifted, a little water to make it into paste, roll it thin, and put it into petty pans; cut the edges even, prick them all over with a pin, and put them in a flow oven; when baked, ice them on the edges and dry them. You may fill them with different sorts of sweet-meats.

290. *To make* TARTS *in Glass Petty Pans*.

Fill them with sweet-meats, roll thin lids as possible, butter the edges of your glasses to make the paste stick; take a skewer and mark them round the edge, wet them over with water, and grate some sugar over them; a very little time will bake them, and do not let your oven be too hot.

291. *To make a* TART.

Roll a sheet of tart paste, put it into your dish, boil up some cramberries with loaf sugar; when cold put them in, and trellice them over with puff paste, cut a border out to lay round your dish, and bake it. You may fill them with any sort of fruit or codlings when they are greened.

292. *To make an* ORANGE PYE.

Take four seville oranges, scrape the out rhind with a pen-knife, cut them in quarters, pick the meat out, and tie them up in a cloth; boil them in spring water 'till tender; then take a pound of double refined sugar, dip it in water, and melt it down, drain the oranges out of the water, and put them into your fyrrup, boil them till they be quite clear, pick all the fkins and feeds out of the pulp, put to it a little fugar, and boil it a little; take a deep difh, the fize you think will do for your oranges, roll out fome tart pafte, butter the edge of your difh, and lay it on, prick it all over, and cut it by the rim of your difh; when it is baked, turn it upon the difh you intend to ferve it on, cut out a lid of puff pafte, the bignefs of your pye, cut out a few figures, and bake with your lid; then make your orange and pulp hot, and pour into your cruft, lay your lid on and the figures.

293. *To make a* CALF'S FOOT PYE.

Take a gang of calf's feet, boil them tender, take out all the bones, and when cold flice them thin; take half a pound of beef fuet fhred fine, a pound of currants clean wafhed and picked, half a pound of raifins ftoned, a little falt, half a lemon peel fhred fine, a quarter of an ounce of cinnamon, half the quantity of mace beat fine, half a pound of fugar, a jack of white wine, half a jack of brandy, half a jack of verjuice, flice a quarter of a pound of orange and citron, mix all well together, butter your difh, lay a rim of pafte round the edge, put in your meat, lid it, but if you let it be over thick it looks clumfy. If

you

you wet the edge of puff paste, it prevents it's rising.

294. *To make* Puffs.

Take a pound of flour, three quarters of a pound of butter, put two ounces in small pieces into the flour, two eggs, a little cold water, make it into paste, roll it out thin, put your butter in at three times, rolling it thin, and dredging it every time; take a dredging box lid, and cut the paste, lay them on a paper, with a little sweetmeat in the middle; cut a lid to lay at the top, the same bigness; do them round the edge with the end of your finger, and bake them in a quick oven, but not to brown them.

295. *To make a* Hare Pye.

Take your hare, wash and wipe it clean, cut it into handsome pieces, and season it with salt, pepper and mace; lay it in your dish, with butter over it, lay a screed of paste round the edge of your dish and lid, and bake it; when it is enough, pour some good brown gravy hot into it. It must be made of puff paste.

296. *To make a* Turkey Pye.

Bone a couple of young turkeys, and season them with salt, pepper and mace; make hot paste, and a crust which you think will hold your turkeys, put them in, wrap one within the other, lay butter over them, and lid your pye; ornament the lid and sides,

and

and bake it; if it be to eat hot, put in good gravy, with afparagus tops, yolks of eggs, and forcemeat-balls; if to eat cold, you muſt cover them over with a clear jelly made of veal.

297. *To make a* PIGEON PYE.

Waſh and trufs your pigeons, feafon them with pepper and falt, put a lump of butter into the bellies, and lay them in your diſh, with butter over them, lay paſte round the edge of your diſh, lid and bake it; when it is enough, pour good gravy into it.

298. *To make a* TURBOT'S HEAD PYE.

Take a middling turbot's head, well cut off, take out the gills, waſh it clean, and feafon it with mace, pepper and falt; put it in your diſh, with half a pound of butter over it, cover it with puff paſte, and bake it; when its enough, diffolve an anchovy in gravy, and a little melted butter, which pour hot into it.

299. *To make an* EEL PYE.

Skin and waſh your eels, cut them in pieces the length of your finger, and feafon them with mace, pepper and falt; lay them in your diſh with butter over them; cover it with puff paſte, and bake it in a gentle oven; when it is enough, pour a little gravy into it.

300. *To make a young* ROOK PYE.

Take what quantity of rooks you think proper, cafe, draw, and waſh them, feafon them

them with pepper and salt, lay them in your dish with forc'd-meat-balls, and butter over them, cover them with cold butter paste, and bake it; when enough, pour a little gravy into it.

301. *An* OLIVE PYE.

Cut some thin slices of a fillet of veal, beat them with a paste-pin, and season them with mace, pepper and salt; make a forc'd-meat, and put the bigness of an egg in every slice, and roll them up; lay them in your dish, and cover them with puff paste; and when baked, lay in yolks of eggs, and pour in some hot gravy.

302. *To make a* RABBET PYE.

Take your rabbets, wipe, and cut them in pieces, lard them with bacon, and season them with mace, pepper and salt, shread a little parsley and sprinkle over them; lay them in your dish with savoury balls, cover them with cold butter paste, and when baked, pour in some good veal gravy.

303. *To make an* OYSTER PYE.

Take a pint of large oysters, clean them in their own liquor, and if you have not liquor enough, take a little water; take a sweet-bread cut in thin slices, season it with a little pepper and salt, lay it in the bottom of your dish, and cover it with the oysters, shread a little marrow, and do over it, cover it with a thin puff paste; when baked, take off the lid, put into it a
lit-

little gravy thickened with butter and flour, and a spoonful of white wine, made hot.

304. *To make a* LOBSTER PYE.

Take lobsters and boil them, take them clean out of the shells, slice the tails and claws thin, and season them with pepper, mace and salt, beat fine; take the bodies, with some oysters, well washed and shread, a little grated bread, some parsley shread, the yolks of raw eggs, mix them well together, and roll them up in balls; lay all into your dish with butter at the bottom and top of the fish, and bake it; pour in sauce of strong gravy, a little oyster liquor strained, a little white wine; thicken it with a little flour and butter, and pour it in hot.

305. *To make a* VENISON PASTY.

Take a side of venison, skin and bone it, cut it to fit your pasty tin, make a paste of half a pound of butter boiled in water, and knead with flour, roll it and put it into your tin, season your venison with mace, pepper and salt, lay it even in; cut it with the point of your knife to prevent its rising, and cover it with pasty paste, if its fresh break the bones, season and put them in a pot with water, and a paper tyed over, and send to the oven; when your pasty is baked, pour in the gravy made from the bones; if they be stale, make gravy of beef.

306. *To make* UMBLE PYE.

Take the umbles of a deer, and parboil them;

them; when they are cold, take half their weight in beef suet and shread them all fine, adding half a pound of sugar; season with mace, nutmeg and salt, a pint of canary, and two pounds of currants wash and picked, mix all well together. You may bake it in a raised crust, or in a dish.

307. *To make a* BEEF-STAKE PYE.

Take rump stakes, beat them with a paste-pin, and season them with pepper and salt; fill your dish, cover it with cold butter paste, and when baked put in gravy.

308. *To make a* GREEN GOOSE PYE.

Bone your goose, and season it with pepper, salt and nutmeg; raise your crust just to hold your goose, put it in, lay butter over, and lid it; cut some figures out of your paste to ornament the top and sides; when baked, pour gravy in, so serve it hot.

309. *To make a* SWAN PYE.

After skinning and boning your swan, lard it with bacon, and season it with pepper, salt, cloves, mace and nutmeg, to your palate, lay it in the pye, stick it with cloves, lay on some butter, and close it; when it is baked, and almost cold, fill it up with clarified butter.

310. *To make a* PHEASANT PYE.

Draw your pheasant, and season it with pepper and salt to your taste, make a forc'd-meat of veal and stuff the body with it; having raised your pye, lay a layer of butter in the bottom, put in your pheasant with a layer of butter on the top, and some of your forc'd-meat that was left lay round it; then lid your pye and bake it; when its drawn, cut up the lid, and put into it a ragoo; so serve it.

311. *To make a* FAWN PYE.

First bone the fawn, then lard it very thick with bacon, and season it with pepper, salt, mace and nutmeg; put some savoury forc'd-meat into the belly, lay it together in the form it was before boned, raise your pye of hot paste in the form of it, and lay it in so that it do not break down the sides; lay butter over, and lid it, and when baked and cold, pour in clarified butter. Any thing that is to be eat cold requires more seasoning than when used hot.

312. *To make a Yorkshire* CHRISTMAS PYE.

Raise a pretty strong crust, bone a goose, a turkey, a fowl, a partridge, and a pigeon, season them with half an ounce of mace, half an ounce of nutmegs, an equal quantity of salt, half an ounce of white pepper, all beat fine together, wrap them one within another, and the goose on the outside; lay them in the crust, so as to look like one goose; take a hare wiped clean with a cloth; cut it in pieces, and lay it as close as you can on one side, and on the other woodcock, more or ., or what sort of wild fowl you can get, season them well, and put butter over

over them; then lay on a thick lid, and let it be well baked; when its taken out of the oven, fill it with clarified butter: before you put it into the oven, take some strong paper doubled and buttered to bind about the sides, which is a great support to a raised crust, and keeps the ornaments from burning.

313. *To make a* Goose Pye.

Take two geese at Christmas, cut them down the backs, and take out all the bones, season them well with mace, pepper, salt and nutmeg; wrap one within the other, and raise a crust that will just hold them, lay them in, run the knife point into the skin in several places, to prevent them rising; put butter over, and lid it, and when baked, pour in clarified butter. This is a real goose pye, and preferable to such a medley as the above.

314. *To make a* Bride Pye.

Parboil cocks-combs, lamb-stones, and veal sweet breads, blanch ox-palates, and cut them in slices; add to them a pint of oysters, slices of interlarded bacon, some blanched chesnuts, a handful of pine kernels, and some dates sliced; season them with salt, nutmeg and mace, and fill your pye with them; lay slices of butter over them, and close it up; when baked, take veal gravy, a spoonful of white wine, a little butter rolled in flour, made hot, and pour it in; so serve it up.

315. To make a LARK PYE.

Take two dozen of larks, lay between every one a little bacon, and a leaf of sage; put a little forc'd-meat in their bellies, and lay them in your crust, lid and bake it one hour; when enough, thicken and pour in some gravy; so serve it hot.

316. To make a CALF's CHALDRON PYE.

Take a calf's chaldron, clean and boil it, set it by to cool, and when cold, chop it very fine with half a pound of marrow, season it with pepper and salt, adding the juice of half a lemon, mix all together; sheet your dish with puff paste, put in your meat, and lid and bake it.

317. To make CALF's HEAD PYE.

Cleanse and wash your head very well, boil it, blanch the tongue and cut all in slices, and cut the eyes in two; scald a pint of oysters, wash and beard them, take the yolks of six eggs, intermix some slices of bacon with them, seasoned with pepper and salt, lay them on your dish, put in a little of the liquor that the head was boiled in, cover it with puff paste, and bake it; when enough, put in gravy, and serve it up.

318. To make an APPLE PYE.

Pare and score your apples, cut them in slices, put sugar in your dish, lay in your apples, a little shread lemon peel, and a gill of white wine. You may cover it with puff or tart paste, whether you please.

319. To

319. *To make* Minced Pies.

Take a gang of calf's feet, boil them, and take out the bones; when cold, chop them on a block, with half a pound of beef suet, a pound of apple shread with them, a little lemon-peel shread fine, a pound and half of currants washed and picked, a quarter of an ounce of cinnamon, half the quantity of mace beat fine, half a pound of sugar, a jack of white wine, half a jack of brandy, a jack of verjuice, a little salt, mix all well together; you may add a quarter of a pound of candid orange cut in slices; sheet your petty-pans with puff paste, fill and lid them; do not wet the edges; bake them in a quick oven, but not to be brown. If you do not use all your meat, put it well down in a pot and tie a paper over it, it will keep good for a week in a cool place, put a little more wet to it when you use it.

320. *To make a* Beef Pasty.

Take a small rump or surloin of beef, bone and beat it with a paste pin; to five pounds of this meat, take three ounces of sugar, rubbed well in, let it lay twenty four hours, wash it with a little claret, and season it well with salt, pepper and nutmeg; put it into your pasty tin, with a sheet of paste in the bottom, and cover it with cold butter paste, and bake it; put the bones into a pot with water, and bake them to make gravy; when baked, put in a little of the gravy.

321. *To make a* HAM PYE.

Take your ham, lay it in water forty-eight hours, cut the shank off, trim and half boil it; take off the skin, stuff the ham with chopt parsley and sage all over, and lay on the skins; have ready a raised crust that will hold it, put in your ham, and bake it, and when baked, take the skin off.

322. *To make a* CHICKEN PYE.

Take as many chickens as you think proper, truss, and season them with pepper and salt, shread a little parsley, work it in butter, and put into their bellies, lay them in your pye, with some forc'd-meat balls, lay butter over, lid, and bake it, and when baked, take veal gravy, oysters, a sweet-bread shread, and thicken it with butter and flour, a little juice of lemon, make it hot, and pour it in; serve it up without lid.

323. *To make* EGG PIES.

Take the yolks of eight hard eggs, and their weight of beef suet, all minced fine, put in a pound of currants, a quarter of a pound of dates stoned and sliced, some beaten spice, lemon-peel, rose-water and sugar, a little salt, mix all well together, and fill your pies; sheet your tins with puff paste, and you may add a little canary.

324. *To make* PATTIES.

Roll out a sheet of puff paste, cut some leaves

leaves round, or in what shape you please, put oysters in some, and forc'd-meat in others; lay paste on the top, and finger them round, lay them on paper, and bake them; they are pretty garnish for fricaseys or made dishes.

325. *To make* GOOSEBERRY TARTS.

Take tart paste, rolled thin, sheet your petty-pans, and lay in a little sugar; take young gooseberries, lay in one layer of gooseberries, and sugar on the top; wet the edges and roll the lids out as thin as possible, finger them round, and bake them; when you put them into the oven, wet them on the top with water, and grate sugar over them.

326. *To keep* GOOSEBERRIES *for* TARTS.

Take gooseberries before they are full grown, wipe and pick them one by one, put them into wide mouthed bottles, cork them close, and set them in a slow oven till they are tender and cracked; then take them out of the oven, and pitch or rosin the corks.

327. *To keep* DAMSINS *for* TARTS.

Wipe your damsins, put them in an earthen pot, and as you lay them in, between every layer strew in beaten loaf-sugar; two pounds of sugar will do for six pounds of damsins; when you have filled the pot, tie a paper over it, and put it into the oven; do not bake them over much; after they are drawn, let them stand till cold; render mutton suet and pour it over them, tie a bladder over, and let them stand in a cold place.

328 *To keep* Cramberries *for* Tarts.

Take cramberries when they are near ripe, pick the decay'd ones and stalks out; take bottles that have been dried sometime in the sun, fill and cork them close down, and rosin the corks. You may keep bullace, currants, and damsins, the same way.

329. *To keep* Figs *all the Year.*

Take a large earthen pot, put the fruit into it in layers, with their own leaves betwixt each layer, boil up water and honey, skimming it till no more will arise, but do not make it too thick of the honey, pour it in warm to them, stop up the pot close; when you take them out for use, put them in warm water, and they will have almost their natural taste.

330. *To keep* Strawberries, Raspberries, *and* Mulberries.

Take new stone bottles, air them well in the sun, or by the fire, dry your fruit to prevent its sweating, take off the stalks, and put them into the bottles by the fire; cork them close, and set them in a cool place.

331. *To keep* Grapes, Apricots, Peaches, *and* Plumes.

Pull your fruit when near ripe, dip the ends of their stalks in melted bees-wax, dry your fruit in the sun, having a large ash box with a lid to shut close down, strew a layer of of millet-seed, and a layer of fruit, let not the fruit touch one another; lay on millet again very even an inch thick, and do so 'till the box is filled, then shut down the lid close; as you take them out, lay them even again. You may keep them in this manner till new ones come again; put them in warm water to plump them if wrinkled.

332. *To make a* RICE PUDDING.

Take half a pound of grinded rice, boil it in three pints of milk, when its as thick as hasty pudding, pour it into a bowl; put in half a pound of butter, stir it till it is melted, a little salt, half a pound of sugar, scrape in the out rhind of two lemons; when its cold, beat and put in six eggs, mix it well up, and bake it with puff paste round your dish.

333. *To make a* CARROT PUDDING.

Take the crumbs of a penny loaf, and scald it with milk to be stiff; grate two middling carrots fine, a spoonful of orange flower water, half a pound of clarified butter, a little salt, and half a nutmeg, six eggs well beat, and sugar to your palate; do puff paste round, mix all well together, and bake it; *for sauce,* use wine, butter, and sugar.

334. *To make an* ORANGE PUDDING.

Take the peel of six oranges pared, that no whites do appear, boil them tender, shifting the water in the boiling, beat them in a mortar very fine, scald a quarter of a pound of Naples biscuits with cream, rub them thro' a cullender, half a pound of clarified butter, half a pound of loaf sugar, and six eggs, beat all well together; sheet your dish with puff paste, and pour it into your dish, and bake it.

335. *To make a* CALF'S FOOT PUDDING.

Take two gangs of calf's feet, boil them tender; when cold, shread them fine, take a quarter of a pound of beef suet shread, the crumbs of a penny loaf, a quarter of a pound of sugar, half a pound of currants, half a pound of raisins stoned, add mace, cinnamon and salt, a little lemon peel shread, a spoonful of flour, a glass of brandy, four eggs, mix all well together; butter your cloth, and tye it close; an hour will boil it; when you serve it, stick it with candid orange, and use wine, butter and sugar, for sauce.

336. *To make a* MARROW PUDDING.

Take the marrow of three bones, slice it in thin pieces; take a penny loaf, pare off the crusts, and slice it thin, stone half a pound of raisins of the sun, a quarter of a pound of currants washed, lay paste round the edge of your dish, so lay a layer of marrow, of bread, and of fruit, 'till the dish be full; then have ready a quart of cream boiled with a stick of cinnamon, five eggs beat and mix'd with it, a little nutmeg, and half a pound of sugar; when you are going

ing to put it into the oven, pour in your cream and eggs, and bake it half an hour; when it is drawn, scrape on it sugar, and serve it up.

337. *To make a* Gooseberry Pudding.

Take a quart of green gooseberries, pick and scald them, bruise and rub them thro' a hair sieve, take six spoonfuls of pulp, six eggs, half a pound of sugar, half a pound of melted butter, a handful of bread-crumbs, mix all well together, and bake it with paste round the dish; when you serve it up, grate sugar over it.

338. *To make a* Raspberry Pudding.

Take four Naples biscuits, scald them with a gill of cream, take a pint of raspberries and bruise them thro' a hair sieve, beat four eggs, sweeten all to your taste, mix them well together; sheet your dish with thin paste, and bake it in a gentle oven.

339. *To make an* Apple Pudding.

Pare, score, and coddle six codlings, take the pulp, six eggs, half a pound of sugar, a little lemon peel shread, a few bread crumbs, half a pound of butter, and mix altogether; lay puff paste round your dish, and bake it.

340. *To make a* Millet Pudding.

Take half a pound of millet seed, after its washed and picked clean, take two quarts of milk, some nutmeg grated, half a pound of sugar, mix altogether, pour it into your dish, break in half a pound of butter, and bake it.

341. A Hunting Pudding.

Take a pound of fine flour, a pound of beef suet shread fine, three quarters of a pound of currants washed and picked, a quarter of a pound of raisins stoned and shread, five eggs beat, a little lemon peel, half a nutmeg grated, a gill of cream, a little salt, a little sugar, a glass of brandy, mix altogether, tie it up tight in a cloth, and boil it two hours; have wine, butter, and sugar, for sauce.

342. To make an Apricot Pudding.

Coddle six large apricots tender, bruise them small, and when cold, add six yolks, and two whites of eggs, and a little cream, sweeten it to your taste; put puff paste in your dish, and bake it half an hour in a slow oven; serve it up with grated sugar.

343. To make a Ratifia Pudding.

Boil four laurel leaves in a quart of cream, take them out, and grate in half a pound of Naples biscuit, half a pound of butter, a little salt, nutmeg and sack, take it off the fire, and cover it; when cold, put in two ounces of almonds blanched and beaten, four eggs, mix altogether, and bake it half an hour.

344. To make a Potatoe Pudding.

Take two pounds of white potatoes, boil and peel them, beat them in a mortar, with half

half a pound of butter, a gill of cream, six eggs, half a pound of sugar, a jack of sack, a little salt and nutmeg, half a pound of currants washed and dried, mix altogether, and bake it half an hour in a quick oven.

345. *To make a* QUAKING PUDDING.

Beat eight eggs very well, take three spoonfuls of flour, and a little salt; boil three gills of cream with a stick of cinnamon, and when cold, mix with your eggs and flour; butter your cloth, and do not give it over much room; boil it half an hour, turning it in the water; serve it up with butter. You may stick it with almonds, if you please.

346. *To make a* LEMON PUDDING.

Grate the out side of two lemons, and four Naple biscuits, take six eggs, a gill of cream, half a pound of sugar, half a pound of butter melted, mix all well together, and pour it in; put a sheet of paste in your dish, grate sugar over, and bake it.

347. *To make an* ALMOND PUDDING.

Take a pound of almonds, blanch'd and beat, a pound of butter, a pound of sugar, and beat all well together; take twelve eggs, scrape in the rhind of two lemons, and the juice of half a one; sheet your dish with puff paste, pour all in, and bake it.

348. *To make a* Wine Pudding.

Heat a pint of sherry, with cinnamon and lemon-peel; grate four ounces of biscuits, six eggs beaten with a little orange flower water, and a little salt and sugar, a little marrow and currants; bake it a quarter of an hour, and when you serve it up, strew sugar over it.

349. *To make a* Quince Pudding.

Scald your quinces very tender, scrape off the pulp, put in powdered sugar, ginger and cinnamon, a pint of cream, and four yolks of eggs; it must be thick of your quinces, butter your dish, and bake it.

350. *To make a* Pudding *of* Plumb Cake.

Slice a pound of plumb cake into a quart of milk, boil and keep stirring it; when its cold, beat four eggs, and put to it a little salt, sugar and some pieces of marrow, mix all well together, and bake it.

351. *A* Beggar's Pudding.

Take some stale bread, put over it some hot water 'till its well soaked; then press out the water, and mash the bread, add some powdered ginger, and grated nutmeg, a little salt, sack, sugar and currants, mix these well together, and lay it into a pan well buttered on the sides, flatting it well with a spoon; lay some butter on the top, bake it in a gentle oven, and serve it up hot, with grated sugar over it. You may turn it out of the pan when its cold, and it will eat like a cheese-cake.

352. *To make a* RYE BREAD PUDDING.

Take half a pound of sour rye-bread grated, half a pound of beef suet shread fine, half a pound of currants clean washed, half a pound of sugar, some nutmeg grated, mix all well together, with six eggs; boil it an hour, and serve it up with melted butter.

353. *To make a* PIPPIN PUDDING.

Make a good puff paste, rolled half an inch thick, pare your apples and score them, put them in the paste and close it up, tie it in a cloth and boil it; a middling sized pudding will take an hour and a half in boiling; when its enough, turn it out on your dish, cut a piece out of the top, and butter and sugar it to your taste; lay on the top again, and send it to the table hot.

354. *To make an* HERB PUDDING.

Take a good quantity of parsley and spinage, a little thyme and marrygold flowers, put to them a gill of creed oat-meal, shread them very small with a little beef suet, a few crumbs of bread, a gill of cream, four eggs, and a little salt, mix all very well together, dredge your cloth, and tye it close; it will take a great deal of boiling.

355. *To make a* CUSTARD PUDDING.

Take a pint of cream, mix with it six eggs, two spoonfuls of flour, half a nutmeg grated ed, a little salt and sugar to your taste, butter a cloth, put it in when the pot boils, and boil it half an hour; *for sauce,* use melted butter.

356. *To make an* OAT-MEAL PUDDING.

Take a pint of groats, a pound of suet shread fine, the like quantity of currants, half as many raisins, mix all together with a little salt, tie it in a cloth, allowing room for its swelling, and boil it three hours.

357. *To make* PUDDINGS *of different Colours.*

Scald your grated bread with a pint of cream, when cold beat six eggs, half a nutmeg, a little salt, a quarter of a pound of sugar, divide it into six parts, colour one with cochineal, one with juice of spinage, one with syrrup of violets, one with saffron, one with currants, and the other plain; dip your cloths in water, butter and dredge them, put in your puddings, tie them close, and boil them for half an hour; when enough, the plain one in the middle, and lay the others round; *for sauce,* use butter, sack and sugar.

358. *To make a* STAKE PUDDING.

Take a quartern of flour, two pounds of beef suet shread fine, a little salt, mix them with water into a stiff paste, roll it of a moderate thickness; take mutton or beef stakes, season them with pepper and salt, make it up as you do an apple pudding,

tied

tied up in a cloth; if it be a small pudding, two hours will boil it.

359. *To make* PUDDINGS *in Skins*.

Take as many codlings as will do for your dish, make a little hole at the small end, and scoup out all the meat, tho' not over thin; prepare a pudding, either of rice or almonds, as in the former receipt; fill your apples with it, butter a deep dish, put them in, and bake them; when enough, take them with care out of your dish, put them on another, and dredge sugar over them; *for sauce,* use wine, butter and sugar.

360. *To make* BLACK PUDDINGS *in Skins*.

Take two quarts of blood, strain it thro' a sieve, add to it a quartern of creed groats, the crumbs of a penny loaf, a pint of cream, and six eggs beaten; season with pepper, salt, and grated nutmeg, some thyme and winter savoury rubbed fine, mix all well together; shread beef suet, some in square, and some in fine pieces, which makes them lighter; take your skins, and tie them at one end before you begin, do not fill them over full; as they are boiling prick them with a pin to prevent their breaking, and when enough, smother them up in straw; when you have filled part, put in more suet and seasoning.

361. *To make* WHITE PUDDINGS *in Skins*.

Take a pound of marrow or beef suet shread fine, three quarters of a pound of
grated

grated bread, boil a pint of cream, and pour upon them; then take a pound of Jordan almonds beaten fine with rose-water, a little salt, half an ounce of mace and cinnamon beaten fine, eight eggs, a pound of sugar, and a gill of sack, mix altogether; fill your skins but half full, put in a little citron as you fill them, tie them up in links, and boil them a quarter of an hour. You may put currants in some, if you please.

362. *To make a* TANSEY.

Take the crumbs of a penny-loaf, and scald it with cream; then take a quarter of a pound of sugar, six eggs, a little salt, a quarter of a pound of butter, mix all well together; green it with the juice of spinage and tansey, butter a paper, lay it in a deep dish, pour in your tansey, and set it in the oven; when enough, turn it up on your dish, take the paper off, and cut an orange in quarters, and lay round; have wine, and sugar in a boat.

363. *To make* PLUMB DUMPLINS.

Take a pound of flour, half a pound of beef suet shread fine, a quarter of a pound of butter, an egg, a little milk, a little salt, make it up into paste, divide it in two, tie them up in a cloth, and they will take three hours boiling. You may put currants in one half, and leave the other plain.

364. *To make* DROP DUMPLINS.

Take a gill of milk, two eggs, a little salt,

salt, and make it into a thick batter with flour; have ready a pan of boiling water, drop in your batter, four minutes will boil them, be sure the water boils quick, drain them from the water, lay them on the dish, and eat them with butter.

365. *To make* APPLE DUMPLINS.

Pare some large apples, cut them in quarters, take out the cores, take a piece of puff paste, roll it big enough for one apple, and close them up round like a ball; tie each dumplin single in a cloth, and put them in boiling water three quarters of an hour; when they are enough, serve them with butter and sugar.

366. *To make* PANCAKES *called a Quire of Paper*.

Take a pint of cream, a quarter of a pound of melted butter, three spoonfuls of flour, a spoonful of orange flower water, a little sugar, and a nutmeg grated, mix all together with eight eggs, leaving out two of the whites; mix your flour at first with a little of it, to make it smooth; butter your pan for the first pancake, and let it run as thin as you can to be whole, when one side is coloured, its enough, take it carefully out of the pan, sift on each some fine sugar beaten, lay them as even on each other as you can; this quantity will make twenty.

367. *To make* CLARY PANCAKES.

Beat twelve eggs very well, with a little salt,

salt, put in five or six spoonfuls of flour, mix them well together till they are very smooth; then put in a pint of milk, melt three or four ounces of butter, pour it into the batter, stir it all the time you are pouring it in, and mix all well together; have ready as much young clary picked, washed, and shread as you think fit; put the bigness of a hasle nut of butter into your pan, and make it hot before you put in your batter to fry them.

368. *To make* CREAM PANCAKES.

Take a pint of cream, eight eggs, a nutmeg grated, a little sack, and a little salt; melt a pound of butter, and before you fry them stir it in; make it as thick with flour as ordinary batter, and fry them with butter; in the first pancake only strew sugar, turn it on the back-side of a plate. Garnish with orange.

369. *To make* PANCAKES *Royal*.

Take half a pint of cream, half a pint of sack, the yolks of eighteen eggs, half a pound of fine sugar, with beaten cinnamon, and nutmeg, mix all well together; then put in as much flour as will make it stiff enough to spread thin over your pan; let the pan be hot, and fry them in clarified butter; they will not be crisp, but are very good.

370. *To make* RICE PANCAKES.

Take a quart of cream, three spoonfuls of

of flour of rice, boil them thick, stir in half a pound of butter, and a grated nutmeg; then pour it out into a balon, and when cold, put in three or four spoonfuls of flour, a little salt, some sugar, nine eggs well beaten, mix all well together, and fry them in a little pan, with a small piece of butter; serve up four or five in a dish.

371. *To make* FRENCH MACKROONS.

Take half a pound of flour, the yolks of two eggs, a little water, make them into a paste; roll it out thin, and cut it long and small as a worm; put them into a pan of boiling water; a quarter of an hour will boil them, drain them thro' a cullender, lay them on your dish, and pour sack and sugar over them.

372. *To make* SOLOMONGUNDY.

Mince very fine some white of chicken, or veal, and the yolks of hard eggs all separate, a little hang beef or tongue, and some pickled cucumber shread fine, some parsley and shallot shread; take a china dish that you intend to lay it on, lay a deep plate on your dish the wrong side upwards. You may lay it in what form you like, as a star, a pyramid, or in squares; and you may lay round it capers, anchovy, lemon, and barberries.

373. *To make transparent* SOLOMONGUNDY.

Take six white herrings, lay them in water all night, boil them, and take the fish from the bone, leaving the head, tail, and
bone

bone whole, fhread the meat with anchovies, an apple and fhallots, lay it over the bones on both fides, in the fhape of a herring; then take the peel of a lemon, and cut it in long pieces to cover over the herrings. You may do fome with beet root; lay them on the difh you intend to ferve them in; boil fome ifinglafs in a quart of the water the fifh was boiled with, a bunch of fweet herbs, whole pepper, mace, and a little vinegar, run it thro' a gilly bag, when cold pour it over your fifh, and let it ftand till gellied.

374. *To ftew* PEARS.

Pare your pears and put them into a pewter flaggon, mix a quart of water with a gill of red wine fweetened to your tafte, and a little cinnamon and cloves; put it to your pears, and lay your parings on the top, fhut the lid clofe, and let them ftand in the oven all night. You may put in a little cochineal tied in a rag, to make them a better colour, if you pleafe.

375. *To ftew* RED CABBAGE.

Take your cabbage and cut it fine, leaving out the large veins, boil it till tender, and drain it; then put it into a fauce-pan with a little melted butter, two fpoonfuls of vinegar, a little pepper and falt, two fpoonfuls of gravy, keep it ftirring over your ftove fix minutes, then ferve it up hot with fryed faucefages round it.

376. STEW-

376. Stewed Sellery.

Take your sellery, wash, and cut it an inch long, and boil it in salt and water till tender; then drain it, and put in a little gravy, melted butter, cream, pepper and salt, and serve it up hot.

377. Stewed Cucumbers.

Take half a dozen cucumbers, pare and cut them in four, length ways, take out the seeds, and put them in water as you do them; have ready some boiling water and salt in a stew-pan, and put them in; let them boil till tender, then drain them, and put them into a little gravy, with a lump of butter wrought in flour, a little mace, pepper and salt; and shake them well together over your stove. You may slice them, if you chuse, and do them after the same manner.

378. *To stew* Mushrooms.

Take your mushrooms, if they are buttons, rub them with a flannel, and put them in milk and water; if flaps, peel, gill, and wash them, put them into your stew-pan, with a little veal gravy, a little mace and salt, thicken'd with a little cream, and the yolks of three eggs; keep it stirring all the time, least it curdle; and serve them hot.

379. *To stew* Parsnips.

Boil them tender, scrape them clean, cut them in slices, and put them into a stew-pan, with cream; shake the stew-pan often, and when

when the cream boils, put in a piece of butter rolled in flour, and pour them upon your dish hot.

380. *To stew* Spinage.

Take your spinage, pick and wash it several times, put it into a sauce-pan, with a little salt over it, and cover the sauce-pan close; do not put in any water, and stir it often; you must have it on a clear quick fire, and as soon as you find the spinage shrinks, and the liquor which comes out of it boils up, its enough; put it into a sieve to drain, and press it; serve it up with melted butter in a boat.

381. *To stew* Lettices.

Let your lettices lie half an hour in water, then take them out and drain them; put them into a pan of boiling water, with a little salt and butter; let them boil 'till they are almost tender, then take them up and drain them well; take some good gravy in your stew-pan, with an anchovy, pepper and salt, put in your lettices, let them stew till tender, and serve them up hot.

382. *To force a* Cabbage.

Parboil a large white cabbage, then take it out to cool, and when cold, cut out the heart, and fill it with forc'd-meat made of sweet-breads, marrow, bread-crumbs, pepper, salt, nutmeg, thyme, and parsley; work it up with egg, put it into your cabbage, and stove it well in gravy an hour, lay it whole

whole on your dish; thicken your sauce and pour it over it, and lay round it slices of broiled bacon.

383. *To stew* Pease.

Take a stew-pan, and butter the inside well, then put in a quart of pease, two gols lettices cut small, four onions, some pepper and salt to your taste; cover the pan close, and let them stew ten minutes; then put in gravy to moisten the whole; let them stew gently a quarter of an hour, shaking the pan, put in half a pound of butter at different times, adding a little flour to thicken; when near enough, take out the onions, and serve it hot.

384. *To dry* Artichoke Bottoms.

Take the largest artichokes you can get when they are at their full growth, boil them as you would do for eating, pull off the leaves, and take out the choke, cut off the stalk as close as you can, lay them on an earthen dish, and set them in a slow oven; when they are dry, put them in paper bags. They are proper for made dishes.

385. *To dry* Pears *or* Pippins.

Take and wipe them clean, run a bodkin in at the eye, and out at the stalk, put them in an earthen pot, with a quart of strong new ale to half a peck; tie double paper over the pots, and bake them; when cold drain them, and lay them on sieves with wide holes to dry in a slow oven.

386. *To boil all Sorts of* Sprouts *and* Cabbages.

All sorts of sprouts and cabbages must be boiled in a good deal of water, with salt and a little butter; let the water boil before you put in the greens; when the stalks are tender, they are enough, and take them off the fire before they lose their colour, drain them, and serve them with butter in a boat.

387. *To boil* Asparagus.

Scrape all the stalks very carefully, till they look white, cut them all even, and tie them in little bunches, put them in a pan of boiling water and salt, and let them boil gently till they are tender, then take them up; make a toast, lay it on the dish, and pour a little butter over it; lay the asparagus all round the dish, with the heads in the middle, and serve it with butter in a boat.

388. *To boil* Kidney Beans.

String and cut them small and long, put them into cold water as you cut them, and when the water boils, put in some salt and the beans; they will be soon boiled, and take care they do not lose their colour; lay them on a plate, and serve them with butter in a boat.

389. *To boil* Artichokes.

Wring off the stalks and put them into cold water, with the tops downwards, that all the sand may boil out; an hour and a quarter will boil them; serve them up with butter in cups.

390. *To boil* BROCOLI.

Strip off all the little branches till you come to the top one, then take a knife and peel off all the hard out-side skin which is on the stalks and little branches, wash them, tie them in little bunches, and boil them in salt and water, with a little butter, the bigness of a walnut; the water must boil before you put them in; they take very little boiling, and if they boil too quick, the heads will come off; when enough, drain them, and serve them with butter in a boat.

391. *To dress* SOUR TROUT.

Take four trout, put it in a pipkin with a lump of butter, cover it close, set it in a pan of boiling water, and let it stand five hours; be sure to keep the water boiling all the time; when enough, serve it with butter in a boat.

392. *To boil* CARROTS.

Wash and boil them, and when enough, peel off the out-side, slice them into a plate, and serve them with butter in a boat; young spring carrots will take half an hour in boiling; if large ones they will take an hour.

393. *To boil* COLLIFLOWERS.

Take off the green part, and either cut them in quarters or boil them whole, lay them an hour in water, then boil them in milk and water skimming it well; when the ftalks are tender, take them carefully up to drain, and serve them up with butter in a boat.

394. *To make* PARSNIP FRITTERS.

Boil your parsnips very tender, flice and beat them in a marble mortar, with a little fine flour, two eggs, a spoonful of cream, some falt, sugar, nutmeg, and two spoonfuls of fack, mix'd all well together, till ftiff. You muft have your pan hot, and drop them in fo as not to touch one another; fry them a light brown on both sides, lay them on your difh, and ftrew fugar over them; *for fauce*, ufe fack and fugar.

395. *To make* APPLE FRITTERS.

Take large apples, pare, core, and cut them in round flices; mix a batter of milk, eggs, flour, nutmeg, fugar, and a little falt and make it fo ftiff as to ftick upon the apple, put the pan over the fire with butter, dip your apples into the batter one by one, lay them into your pan, and fry them a light brown on both fides, fpreading them on a piece of paper before the fire, 'till they are all fryed; lay them on your difh, and ftrew fugar over them; *for fauce*, ufe wine and fugar in a boat.

396. *To make* DROP FRITTERS.

Take a quart of milk, fix eggs, fome falt, and nutmeg, four spoonfuls of ale yeaft, and as much flour as will make a ftiff batter;
then

then take six apples pared and sliced thin, a pound of currants washed, dried, and picked, half a pound of sugar, a glass of brandy, mix all well together, and set them before the fire two or three hours to rise; then have ready a brass pan with clarified butter, drop them in with a spoon, and turn them while they are enough; then take them out, lay them on your dish, and strew sugar over them; *for sauce,* use wine, butter and sugar.

397. *To make* OAT-MEAL FRITTERS.

Boil a quart of milk, put to it a pint of oat-meal flour, and let it steep ten or twelve hours; then beat six eggs, and add a little more milk if there be occasion, to make it of a right stiffness; put some lard in a stew-pan, with a spoonful of batter into it for a fritter; strew some sugar over them, and have sack and butter for sauce.

398. *To make* FRITTERS ROYAL.

Make a posset with a pint of sack, and a quart of milk; take the curd from the posset, put it into a bason, with half a dozen eggs, season it with a little nutmeg, and beat it very well together, adding flour to make the batter a proper thickness; put in some fine sugar, and fry it in clarified beef suet; made hot in the pan before you put the batter in, and serve them up with wine, butter, and sugar.

399. *To make* SKIRRET FRITTERS.

Take a pint of the pulp of skirrets, a spoonful of flour, the yolks of eggs, some sugar and spice, make it of a proper thickness, and fry them with clarified beef suet.

400. *To make a* BACON FRAZE.

Beat eight eggs together with a little cream and flour, like other batter; then fry very thin slices of bacon, and pour some batter over them, and when both sides are fryed, serve them up.

401. *To make* OYSTER *or* COCKLE FRAZE.

Take cockles or oysters, pick them out of their shells, wash them, and break a dozen eggs to a little grated nutmeg, and put to them; beat all well together with a handful of grated bread, and a gill of cream; then put butter into your frying pan, and let it be hot, put in the frazes, supply it with butter in the sides of the pan; let the thin run in the middle, till it moves round; when it is fried on one side, butter your plate, turn it, put it in again, and fry the other side brown; then take it out and dish it, squeeze on the juice of a lemon, and serve it up.

402. *To make* GOOFER WAFERS.

Take a pound of flour, six eggs, beat them very well, put to them about a gill of milk, mix'd very well with the flour, put in half a pound of clarified butter, half a pound of powdered sugar, grate in half a

nut-

nutmeg, and a little salt; you may add to it two or three spoonfuls of cream; then take your goofer irons and put them into the fire to heat, and when they are hot, rub them over with butter in a cloth, put the batter into one side of your goofer irons, and put them into the fire; keep turning the irons, for if they are over hot they will soon burn; make the wafers a day or two before you use them, only set them down before the fire to be hot, before you use them to eat; when you serve them up strew sugar over them; *and for sauce,* use wine, butter and sugar in a boat.

403. *To make* WAFERS.

Take a gill of good cream, a spoonful of orange flower water, some double refined sugar grated to make it pretty sweet, and flour to make it into a pretty thick batter; let it stand by the fire two hours, stirring it some times; then butter your irons the first time.

404. *To make* DUTCH WAFERS.

Take four eggs, and beat them very well; then take a good spoonful of fine sugar, a nutmeg grated, a pint of cream, a pound of flour, a pound of melted butter, two spoonfuls of rose-water, two spoonfuls of yeast, mix all well together, and bake them in your wafer tongs on the fire; *for sauce,* use sack, butter and sugar.

405. To pickle Walnuts.

Take your walnuts when they are so tender that a pin will pass thro' them, and prick them all over, put them in water for four days, shifting them twice a day; make a strong salt and water, put them in a pan, and set it over the fire, cover them with hay till they turn black, but not to be soft, and take them into a sieve to drain; make a pickle of good alegar boiled and skimmed, put in mustard-seed, horse-raddish, ginger, whole-pepper, and shallots, let it have a boil, and pour it on hot.

406. To pickle Walnuts Green.

Take them when tender, pare them thin, and put them into a pan with salt and water, and a little allum; cover them with vine leaves, and hang them over a slow fire 'till they be green, but do not let them boil; put them into a sieve to drain; then take alegar, a few bay leaves, horse-raddish, long pepper, mustard, and shallots, boil them and pour them upon your walnuts, and when cold tie a bladder over them, for air spoils all sorts of pickles.

407. To pickle Mushrooms.

Take button mushrooms, rub them with a piece of flannel, and put them into milk and water; set on your stew-pan with an equal quantity of milk and water, and when it boils put in your mushrooms, and let them boil quick for half a quarter of an hour; pour them into a sieve to drain 'till they are cold;

make

make your pickle of the best white wine vinegar, with mace, whole white pepper, nutmeg sliced, boil it, and when cold, put it to your mushrooms, to cover them, put some sweet oil on the top, and tie a bladder over them.

408. *To pickle* CODLINGS.

Gather green codlings, put them into a pan of water 'till you can peel off the skins; then put vine leaves over them, and hang them over a slow fire 'till they are green; make your pickle of vinegar, a spoonful of salt to each quart, four shallots, a quarter of an ounce of ginger sliced, and a quarter of an ounce of pepper and mace; boil it in a brass pan for eight minutes, drain your codlings, and put them into a stone or glass jar, pour your pickle on hot, and lay a cloth over them 'till cold, then tie them up close.

409. *To pickle* CODLINGS *like* MANGO.

Prepare a brine of salt and water, strong enough to bear an egg, put into it a dozen of the largest full grown, tho' not ripe, codlings you can get, let them lay in this brine nine or ten days, shifting them every other day, dry them with a cloth, and carefully scoup out the cores; the stalks must be taken out so as to fit again, the eye must be left in, and the inside must be filled with sliced ginger, a clove of garlick, mace, horse-raddish, and mustard-seed, put in the stalk, and tie it up tight; make your pickle of of white wine vinegar, and pour it boiling hot on them every other day for a week.

410. *To pickle* WALNUTS *White*.

Take the largest full grown walnuts you can get, prick them thro' with a pin, pare off all the green, and put them in salt and water as you pare them; then boil them in salt and water for eight minutes, and drain them; put them into a pot with as much distilled vinegar as will cover them, and let them lay two days; take as much more vinegar, some blades of mace, and a little white pepper and salt, boil and skim it, and when cold, take your walnuts out of the other pickle and put them into this; put them in bottles, pour on oil, and tie a leather over them.

411. *To pickle* SAMPHIRE.

Take samphire that is green, pick it, and lay it in salt and water for two days, put it into a pan with as much white wine vinegar as will cover it, set it over a slow fire 'till it's green and crisp; then put it into your pot, pour on your pickle, and tie it up close for use.

412. *To pickle* HOPBUDS.

Give them a boil or two in salt and water, and when cold put them in white wine vinegar, and tie them close.

413. *To pickle* COLLIFLOWERS.

Cut the whitest and closest colliflowers, in pieces half the length of your finger, from the

the ſtalks, boil them a little in milk and water, tho' not 'till they are tender; take them out and cool them; for pickle, uſe white wine vinegar, mace, and whole white pepper; give it a boil, and when cold, put in your colliflowers, and tie them up cloſe.

414. *To pickle* COLLIFLOWERS *Red.*

Break the colliflowers in pieces the bigneſs of a muſhroom, leave on a ſhort ſtalk with the head; take a pint of white wine vinegar, two pennyworth of cochineal beaten fine, and tied in a muſlin rag, a little pepper, ſalt and cloves, boil them in your vinegar, preſſing the cochineal with a ſpoon againſt the ſide of your pan as it boils, and pour it hot over them; let it ſtand cloſe covered two days, then you may ſcald it again 'till it be red, and tie it cloſe down with leather. If you chuſe to have them yellow, you muſt uſe ſaffron inſtead of cochineal.

415. *To pickle* KIDNEY BEANS.

Take them when they are young, and ſcald them in ſtrong ſalt and water twice a day till they are green; then make a pickle of alegar, drain your beans out, and waſh them in a little of it, put them into your pots and pour the reſt over them, and when cold, tie them cloſe up.

416. *To pickle* BARBERRIES.

Get barberries when ripe, and put them into a pot; boil ſalt and water and when

cold,

cold, pour it on them, and cover them up close.

417. *To pickle* BEET ROOT.

Take fresh beet, but cut not the ends off, if you do it loses it's colour, boil it in water, salt and vinegar 'till tender; boil some alegar with whole pepper, and when cold slice your beet into it. You may do carrots the same way.

418. *To pickle* MELLONS.

Take young green mellons, cut a piece out of their sides the length of your mellons, take out their seeds, drain and rub the insides with salt; then put into them mustard-seed bruised, shallots and ginger sliced, whole pepper, and horse-raddish; put your pieces in again, tie them fast down, put them in strong salt and water, and hang them over the fire covered close up 'till they are green; make a pickle of white wine vinegar and spices, and take the mellons out of the salt and water, and put them into it when hot, and tie them close down. You may do large cucumbers the same way.

419. *To pickle* GERKINS.

Take your gerkins and rub them with a cloth; make a strong brine of salt and water, put them into a stone jar and pour it upon them boiling hot twice a day for three days, setting them near the fire all the time, then take them out to drain, and make a pickle of vinegar, whole pepper, ginger and dill

dill seed; put them into a jar, and pour the pickle on hot, cover the jar up close, and when cold, put on a bladder.

420. *To pickle* ONIONS.

Peel onions of a small size, put them in water, and just give them a boil, but not to make them tender, and put them into a sieve to drain; make you pickle of vinegar a nutmeg sliced, a little mace, salt and ginger, boil it, and when cold put in your onions, and tie a wet bladder over them.

421. *To pickle* SPANISH ONIONS.

Peel them, cut small round pieces out of the bottoms, and scoup out the insides, but not too thin, put them in salt and water three days, changing it twice a day, then drain them, and stuff them with mustard-flour, sliced ginger, mace and shallot cut small, and scraped horse-raddish, put in the pieces, and tie them fast; make a strong pickle of white wine vinegar, mace, ginger, nutmeg, sliced horse-raddish, and a good deal of salt; put in the mango, let them boil up three times, but take care they do not boil too much for they will loose their firmness; then put them with the pickle into a jar, and cover them down close; the morning after boil your pickle up again, and pour it over them.

422. *To pickle* WHITE CABBAGE.

You may cut it in quarters, or shave it in long slices, scald it six minutes in salt and
wa-

water, and take it out to drain ; boil some vinegar, whole pepper, ginger and mace, put your cabbage into a jar, and pour the pickle on hot, and tie it close down.

423. *To pickle* RED CABBAGE.

Cut off the out leaves and stalks, shave your cabbage in thin long slices, leaving out the white part as much as you can, put it on a dish and strew salt over it, and let it lay for six hours; make your pickle of vinegar, whole pepper, ginger sliced, and nutmeg, boil it, drain your cabbage, and put it into a jar, and when your pickle is cold, pour it upon it.

424. *To pickle* SELLERY.

Cut sellery in pieces two inches in length, with the young tops, boil it in salt and water, and set it to cool in a sieve; boil vinegar, pepper, ginger, and mace, and when cold pour it upon the sellery.

425. *To pickle* FENNEL.

Pick your fennel, tie it in bunches, and just let it boil in salt and water, take it out to drain, put it into a jar, and pour vinegar upon it, with a little mace and nutmeg, and tie leather over it. You may do parsley the same way.

426. *To pickle* RADDISH BUDS.

Gather the youngest buds, and put them in salt and water a day ; then make a pickle of vinegar, cloves, mace, and whole pepper boil'd, drain the buds, and pour the liquor on boiling hot, tie your pot clofe up.

427. *To make* INDIAN PICKLE.

Take a pound of ginger, let it lay in falt and water a night, and cut it in thin flices, then put it in a bowl with dry falt, and let it ftand till the reft of the ingredients are ready; take a pound of garlick peel'd, and cut in pieces, falt it, and let it ftand three days, then wafh and dry it in the fun on a fieve; take cabbages and cut them in quarters, and falt them for three days; then fqueeze out all the water, and fet them two days in the fun, fo do fellery and colliflowers, cut the fellery as far as the white is good, but not thro' the ftalks; raddifhes may be done the fame way, only fcrape them and leave on the young tops; French beans and afparagus lay only two days, then boil them up in falt and water, and do them as the others, take fome long pepper and falt, dry it in the fun, a quarter of a pound of muftard feed, and an ounce of turmerick bruifed fine, put all the above ingredients into a ftone jarr, with a quart of the ftrongeft, and three quarts of fmall vinegar, fill your jarr three quarters full, and look at it in a fortnight, and if occafion, fill it up again. You may do cucumbers, melons, plumbs, apples, carrots, or any thing of this fort; you need never empty the jarr, but as things come in feafon put them in,

being

being all firſt dried in the ſun; keep it filled up with vinegar or freſh pickle.

428. *To pickle* Taragon.

Strip the taragon from the ſtalks, put it into a pot with white-wine and vinegar in equal quantities, ſtop it cloſe up, and keep it for uſe.

429. *Rules to be obſerved in* Pickling.

Always uſe ſtone jarrs for all ſorts of pickles that require hot pickle to them; the firſt charge is the leaſt, for theſe not only laſt longer, but keep the pickle better, as vinegar and ſalt will penetrate through all earthen veſſels, ſtone and glaſs being the only things to keep pickles in. Be ſure never to put your hands into the jarrs to take out the pickles, which ſoon ſpoils them; have a wooden ſpoon, full of holes, to take them out with; let your braſs pans for green pickles be bright and clean, and your pans for white pickles well tinned and clean; otherwiſe your pickles will have no colour; always uſe the ſtrongeſt white wine vinegar; be very exact in watching when your pickles begin to boil and change colour, ſo that you may take them off the fire immediately, otherwiſe they will loſe their colour and grow ſoft in keeping; cover your pickling jarrs with a wet bladder and leather.

430. *To make* Gooseberry Vinegar.

Take gooſeberries when near ripe, and bruiſe them; to every quart of gooſeberries put

put three quarts of water, firſt boiled, and let it ſtand till cold, then put in the berries, and let it ſtand two days; then ſtrain it thro' a bag, and put a pound of brown ſugar to every gallon of liquor, ſtir it well, put it into a barrel, and cover it up. You may either ſet it by the fire, or in the ſun; the warmer it is kept, the ſooner it will be fit for uſe.

431. *To make* ELDER VINEGAR.

Take the beſt white wine vinegar, put to it as many ripe elder berries as you ſhall think fit, in a wide mouthed glaſs, ſtop it cloſe, and ſet it in the ſun a week; then pour it out gently into another glaſs, and keep it for your uſe.

432. *To make* RAISIN VINEGAR.

Take what quantity of water you pleaſe, put it into a veſſel, and to every gallon of water put two pounds of Malaga raiſins, cover your veſſel up, and ſet it in the ſun till it is fit for uſe.

433. *To make* SUGAR VINEGAR.

To every gallon of water, put a pound of coarſe ſugar, let it boil, and ſkim it as long as any ſkim riſes; then pour it into your tub when it is near cold; take a toaſt of brown bread, rub it over with yeaſt, put in your toaſt, and let it work twenty four hours; then put it into your veſſel, cover it up, and ſet it in the ſun; if it ſtands warm, it will be fit to uſe in three months.

434. *To*

434. *To make* WALNUT CATCHUP.

Take them when they are fit for pickling, and beat them in a mortar, strain the juice thro' a flannel bag, and put to each quart of juice, a gill of white wine, a gill of vinegar, a dozen shallots sliced, a quarter of an ounce of mace, two nutmegs sliced, an ounce of black pepper, twenty four cloves, and the peels of two sevile oranges or lemons pared so thin that no white do appear; boil it very well over a gentle fire, and skim it well as it boils; let it stand a week or ten days covered very close, then pour it thro' your bag, and bottle it.

435. *To make* MUSHROOM CATCHUP.

Take a stew-pan, put in some large flapped mushrooms, and the ends of those you wipe for pickling, put it on a slow fire with a handful of salt, but no water, when they are boiled down, press the liquor from them thro' a sieve; to every quart put in two shallots, a quarter of an ounce of mace, half an ounce of black pepper, six cloves, four rases of ginger, boil and skim it very well before you put your spices in, and after they are in, the longer its boiled, the better it will keep; pour it into a pot, cover it, and when cold, bottle it.

436. *To make* MUSHROOM POWDER.

Cut off the stalks of large mushrooms, having washed them clean from grit, but do not peel or gill them, put them in a kettle

over

over the fire, without water, with a good quantity of spice, two shallots peeled, strew them with salt, and a lump of butter, let them stew till all the liquor is dried up, then take them out and dry them, till they will beat to powder; put it into a pot, and tie a cover over it; so keep it for your use.

437. *To make a rich* CATCHUP.

Take a gallon of strong stale ale, a pound of anchovies washed, half an ounce of mace, half an ounce of cloves, half an ounce of pepper, four rases of ginger, a pound of shallots, a quart of large mushrooms well rubbed and picked, boil all over a slow fire, till half wasted, strain it thro' a flannel, and let it stand till cold; then bottle and cork it very close. This is thought to be as good as soyle.

438. *To make* CREAM CHEESE.

Take three quarts of new milk, a quart of cream, a spoonful of earning, and a little salt, let it stand 'till it curdle, then put it into the vat, and three pounds weight upon it; about two hours after, you may lay a six pound weight upon it; turn it often into dry cloths 'till night, then take off the weight and cloth, and let it lay in the vat 'till morning; when it's dry lay it in nettles, turning it 'till fit for use.

439. *To make a* SLIPCOAT CHEESE.

Take five quarts of new milk, and a quart of cream, make it new milk warm and put
in

in your earning ; take your curd and drain it, break it as little as you can, and lay it in a cloth in your cheese vat, cover it, and lay two pounds weight upon it; when it will hold together, turn it out of the vat, and keep turning it 'till it hath done wetting, then lay it upon grafs 'till it is ripe.

440. *To make* Sage Cheese.

Bruise the tops of young red sage and spinage in a mortar, put it into new milk to make it green and taste of the sage, put in your earning, and let it stand 'till it breaks; take the curd and put it into your cheese vat, with a little salt, press it down eight hours; then turn it twice a day for a week, and it will be fit for use.

441. *To make* Ramakins.

Take a quarter of a pound of Cheshire cheese, two ounces of butter, and two eggs, beat them fine in a mortar, and make them up into cakes; lay them in a dish not to touch one another, set them on a chafindish of coals, and hold a salamander over them 'till they be brown, so serve them up hot.

442. *To make a* Scots Rabbet.

Toast a piece of bread on both sides and butter it, cut a piece of cheese the bigness of your bread, toast it on both sides, and lay it on the bread, and serve it up quick.

443. *To make a* Portugal Rabbet.

Toast a slice of bread on both sides, lay it on a plate before the fire, and pour on it a glass a glafs of red wine, let it be foaked up; then cut fome cheefe very thin, and lay it thick over the bread, put it into a tin oven before the fire to brown, and ferve it hot with wine and fugar.

444. *To make an* ITALIAN RABBET.

Toaft a flice of bread and butter it, cut a flice of cheefe, lay it upon your bread, and toaft it with a hot iron, put fome muftard and pepper upon it, and fome anchovies in pieces laid thick over them, fo ferve it up.

445. *To make* ALMOND CHEESE CAKES.

Take half a pound of blanched almonds, half a pound of butter, half a pound of loaf fugar, beat them fine in a mortar, beat fix eggs, and mix all together; fcrape in the out rhind of orange or lemon, fheet your tins with puff pafte, fill your tins half full, and bake them in a quick oven, but not to be brown.

446. *To make* RICE CHEESE CAKES.

Take a quart of cream, a quarter of a pound of ground rice, a ftick of cinnamon, fet it over the fire, and keep ftirring it 'till it be as thick as curd; then pour it into a bowl, and ftir in a quarter of a pound of butter, and half a pound of fugar; and when cold put in four eggs beat, a little falt, and the rhind of a lemon fcraped; fheet your tins with puff pafte, half fill and bake them.

447. *To make* Curd Cheese Cakes.

Take three quarts of new milk, and put to it as much earning as will break it; then drain the curd, and put it in a mortar, with half a pound of butter, a nutmeg grated, and half a pound of sugar, beat them all together with six eggs, a pound of currants, washed, dried and picked, a little salt, and a glass of brandy; sheet your tins with puff-paste, and bake them.

448. *To make* Orange Cheese Cakes.

Boil the peels of three sevile oranges 'till they are tender, changing the water to take off the bitterness, pound them in a mortar with six ounces of loaf sugar, half a pound of butter, four eggs, a spoonful of orange flower water, mix all well together, sheet your tins with puff-paste, half fill them, and bake them in a quick oven. You may make lemon cheese-cakes the same way.

449. *To make an* Almond Custard.

Take a pint of cream, and boil in it a stick of cinnamon; beat the yolks of six eggs, with a spoonful of water, and pour your cream to them stirring them all the time; put all into a pan and set it over the fire, stirring it 'till it be thick, and pour it into a bason; blanch and beat a quarter of a pound of almonds sweetened to your taste, mix all together, and when cold, put in a spoonful of brandy. You may serve it in glasses or in egg shells; your shells must
be

be done thus—break a hole at the thick end of your eggs, pour the egg out, and wash them, dip the outsides in gum-water, do them over with prunella comfits, set them to dry, fill them with custard, and set them in pounded sugar.

450. *To make a* TRIFLE.

Lay mackroons over the bottom of your dish, and pour upon them a glass of sack; then have ready a custard, made pretty stiff, which lay over them. Make a froth of cream, sugar, wine, and juice of lemon, cover your custard over with it, and stick citron in it.

451. *To make* CREAM CURDS.

Take a quart of cream, strain and beat six eggs into it, and mix them well together; set on a pan with three quarts of spring water, when it boils, put in a spoonful of vinegar, and pour in your cream and eggs; as they rise pour in a little cold water, and when they are all risen up, take your pan off the fire, pour them upon a cloth laid in a cullinder, and take them up with a slice to drain.

452. *To make* SAGOE CREAM.

Boil some sifted sagoe in milk three hours, stirring it all the time, put in some cinnamon, and when cold, put in sugar, rosewater, and a glass of sack, so serve it up.

453. *To make a* PLUMB CAKE.

Take four pounds of flour well dried, a
G.   pound,

pound of sugar beaten and searsed, two pounds of butter rubbed fine in your flour, a pint of cream, a pint of yeast, a jack of sack, make them as warm as milk from the cow, beat your yeast well before you put it in, mix all well together, then put in fifteen eggs, strain them thro' a hair sieve; beat your cake very well with the liquids near an hour; have ready six pounds of currants well washed, picked and dried, mix them in hot, with half an ounce of mace, a little salt, half a pound of candid orange, lemon and cittron cut in pretty large pieces, put it in the hoop, and two hours will bake it.

454. *To make a good* Seed Cake.

Take five pounds of flour well dried, four pounds of double refined sugar, beat and sifted, mix them together; then wash four pounds of butter with rose-water, work it with your hand till its like cream; beat and put in twenty eggs, a glass of sack, stirring it with your hand till you put it into the oven, adding before you put it in the hoop, a pound of carraway seeds, half a pound of candid orange and cittron, and a little salt, and back it two hours in a quick oven.

455. *To make a light* Seed-Cake.

Take two pounds of flour, three eggs, a gill of cream, two spoonfuls of yeast, half a pound of butter, half a pound of sugar, four ounces of carraway seeds, a little salt, work all warm together with your hand, butter your tin and bake it. 456. *To*

456. *To make a* Pound Cake.

Take a pound of butter work'd with your hand, eight eggs beat, work them together 'till they are like cream, put in a pound of sugar sifted, a pound of flour, a quarter of an ounce of mace shread, a little salt, a pound of currants, washed, picked and dried, beat it 'till it's white before you put in the currants, and bake it in a quick oven. You may add to it almonds, and suckit if you please.

457. *To make* Iceing *for* Cakes.

Take six whites of eggs beat to a froth, two pounds of double refined sugar searsed, beat it with your eggs 'till they be as white as snow; you may put in a spoonful of rosewater; when your cake comes warm from the oven, rub it well over with a cloth, ice it, and set it to dry.

458. *To make* Queencakes.

Take a pound of butter, and work it with your hand 'till it be as thick as cream; put in eight eggs, a pound of sugar beat and sifted, beat it very well with a thible; put in a pound of flour, a quarter of an ounce of mace shread fine, and a little salt, beat 'till it's white; have ready half a pound of currants washed, picked and dried, butter your tins, and fill them with one half of it; mix your currants in the other half, fill your tins with it, and bake them in a quick oven.

459. *To make* Little Plumb-Cakes.

Take four pounds of flour, a pound of

butter melted in a quart of cream, a pint of yeast, eight eggs, half a jack of sack, a nutmeg grated, a little salt, half a pound of sugar, two pounds of currants cleaned and dried, mix all together, and set it before the fire to rise; butter your tins, and bake them.

460. *To make a* GINGER CAKE.

Take six eggs, a pound and a half of sugar, a pound of butter, two pounds of treacle, a jack of brandy, a quarter of a pound of candid lemon, a pennyworth of ginger, and a few corriander seeds, beat all well together for an hour; then put in as much flour as will make it stiff enough to beat; cover it with flour, and let it stand all night; next day work it together, butter your tin, and send it to the oven.

461. *To make* RED GINGERBREAD.

Take six penny grated white loaves, set them before the fire to dry, and beat and sift them; take three pints of ale, three pounds of brown sugar, a quarter of a pound of beaten ginger sifted, a small handful of anniseeds, half an ounce of cloves, a little mace, a nutmeg, an ounce of cinnamon, two pennyworth of red saunders, and half a pound of beaten almonds; set on your ale and sugar in a pretty large pan, and when it rises, stir it, put in your bread and spice, and let it boil to a paste; take it off the fire, and put in your almonds and a little brandy, then take it up up and work it in; you must put a little of your cinnamon with your other spices, and keep the rest to work it up when you print it.

462. *To make* WHITE GINGERBREAD.

Take half a pound of Jordan almonds blanched in cold water, beat them in a marble mortar very fine, with a little rose-water; take the white of an egg beat to a froth, as much double-refined sugar sifted as will make it a stiff-paste, six-pennyworth of oil of cinnamon dropped on a lump of sugar, beat them also to a good stiff paste. Print it, work it very thin, and keep it dry.

463 *To make* GINGERBREAD.

Take a pound of treacle, half a pound of butter, half a pound of sugar, two pennyworth of cloves, an end of a candid orange cut into slices, and as much flour as will make it into paste, make it in rolls, and bake it on wafers.

464. *To make* YARM CAKES.

Take a pound and a half of butter, slice it thin, and set it in a stone bowl near the fire, 'till it is so soft that you may beat it with your hand as thick as melted butter; then work to it as much fine dried flour as will make it into a light paste, put in two nutmegs grated, some lemon-peel or citron shread small, half a pound of sugar beat fine, a pound of currants, washed, picked and dried, and two spoonfuls of yeast, mix them all together,

ther, lie them upon paper, and grate fine sugar upon them; set them in the oven, and a little time will bake them; take care you do not break them in taking them off the papers, as they are very short. Keep them very dry. This quantity will make forty cakes.

465. *To make* CRACKNELS.

Take half a pound of flour, half a pound of sugar, two ounces of butter, two eggs, and a few carraway seeds, beat and sift the sugar, then put it to the flour, work it to a paste, and roll them as thin as you can; you may cut them out with tins, lay them on papers, and bake them in a slow oven.

466. *To make* SHREWSBERRY CAKES.

Take two pounds of flour, and rub a pound and a quarter of butter well into it; put in a pound and a quarter of fine sugar beaten and sifted, a nutmeg grated, and three eggs beat with a little rose-water, so knead your paste with it, and let it lie an hour; then make it up into cakes, prick them, and bake them on tins wetted with a feather dipped in rose-water; grate sugar over them, and bake them in a slow oven.

467. *To make* WIGGS.

Take a pound of flour, half a pound of butter melted in a jill of cream, two eggs, a spoonful of yeast, a few carraway seeds, a little salt, work them to a paste, and set them an hour to rise; then take half a pound

pound of sugar, make them up into wiggs with it, and bake them on tins.

468. *To make* Sugar Cakes.

Take a pound of sugar beaten fine and sifted, mix with it three quarts of flour, and break in a pound and a quarter of butter; then beat the yolks of four eggs with two spoonfuls of rose-water, and a gill of cream; strain it thro' a sieve, and knead all into a paste, cut your cakes out with a tin, and bake them upon paper in a gentle oven.

469. *To make* Buns.

Take two pounds of flour, a pint of ale yeast, three eggs, a little sack, nutmeg and salt, strain your liquids thro' a sieve into a little warm milk, and make it into a paste; set it before the fire to rise, then knead in a pound of butter, and a pound of carraway comfits, bake them on papers, in a quick oven, in what shape you please.

470. *To make* Poor Knights *of* Windsor.

Take a French roll, cut it into slices, and soak it in sack; then dip them in the yolks of eggs, and fry them; serve them up with butter, sack and sugar.

471. *To make a* Biscuit Cake.

Take nine eggs, a spoonful of rose-water, and a pound of loaf-sugar beaten and sifted, beat them together half an hour; then put in a pound of flour, an ounce of carraway seeds, beat them well, butter your tin, and bake it in a quick oven.

472. *To*

472. *To make* a Common Cake.

Take a pound of flour, half a pound of butter, half a pound of sugar, four eggs, a little milk, an ounce of carraway-seeds, beat it very well, and bake it in a quick oven.

473. *To make* Cakes *to keep all the Year.*

Take a pound and four ounces of flour well dried, a pound of butter unsalted, a pound of beaten sugar, a glass of sack, the rhind of an orange boiled tender; beat some sugar, a nutmeg grated, and four eggs, beat them all well together before you put in your flour, and make it into little cakes; wet the tops with sack and strew on fine sugar; bake them on papers buttered and dredged with flour. You may add a pound of currants washed, dried, picked and warmed.

474. *To make* Mackroons.

Take a pound of almonds, blanch and put them in water, drain, wipe, and put them in a mortar, and beat them, (but not too fine,) with the white of an egg, or a little orange flower water, add to them a pound of sugar beaten and sifted, five eggs, a handful of flour, mix all together, lay them on wafers, and bake them in a gentle oven.

475. *To make* French Bread.

Take half a peck of flour, six eggs well beaten, a pint of light yeast, and as much cream and milk as will make it into paste,

adding

adding a little salt; have the oven ready, and let it lay but a little before you make it into rolls, and bake it.

476. *To make* CRIMSON BISCUITS.

Take the root of red beet, boil it tender, and beat it in a mortar with sifted sugar, some butter, a little flour, the yolks of hard eggs, a little cinnamon beaten, a little orange flower water, and the juice of half a lemon, mix them all together, make them into cakes, and bake them.

477. *To make* ALMOND JUMBALLS.

Take a pound of almonds, blanch and beat them with rose-water; then put to them the whites of four eggs, beat to a froth; stir in three quarters of a pound of double refined sugar searsed, set it over a chafingdish of coals, and dry it till it will work into what shape you please; when its cold, roll it thin with fine searsed sugar and gumdragon steeped in rose-water, in pieces the length of your finger, and broad enough to cover the balls round, then wet and lay your rolls on, and close it handsomely, and to make it less seen when its joined, roll it smaller after its covered; set them to dry where there is a moderate heat, and when dry, put them in boxes, and keep them in a dry place.

478. *To make the* RED COLOURING.

Take an ounce of cochineal, a quarter of an ounce of roach-allum, and two drachms of cream of tartar, pound them in a mortar, and put them into a sauce-pan with a gill and half of water, and let it boil till one third is wasted, then strain it thro' a cloth, and put in two ounces of double refined sugar; put it in a phial, and cork it close; a little of this will do for colouring flummery, iceing, or any thing you please; it will keep good a long while.

479. *To make* Green Colouring.

Take a quarter of an ounce of gambooge, and the same quantity of indico, beat them fine in a mortar, put them in a bottle with two spoonfuls of water, cork it up, and shake it; a few drops of this will colour any thing green.

480. *To make* Cupid's Hedge-Hogs.

Take half a pound of Jordan almonds, and rub them with a cloth to take off all the brown dust; prepare an iceing for them made of half a pound of double refined sugar, beat and searsed, the whites of two eggs, beat with a little more sugar, beat it till its as white as snow and stiff, then take a pin and prick it into the thick end of an almond, and do it all over with your iceing with a knife; then strinkle it all over with prunella comfits, and put it carefully on to a dish; continue doing so till you have made your quantity, and dry them; when they are dry lay them in a box, in a dry place, with paper betwixt them, to keep them separate. You may

may colour a little of the iceing with the former colouring, if you pleafe.

481. *To make a* HEDGE HOG.

Take a pound of Jordan almonds blanched and beat very well in a mortar, with a fpoonful of fack, make them into a ftiff pafte; then beat fix yolks and two whites of eggs, and add to them a jill of cream, a quarter of a pound of butter fweetened to your tafte, fet it on a ftove and keep ftirring it till it be fo ftiff that you may make it into the fafhion of a hedge hog; then ftick it full of blanched almonds, flit and ftuck up like briftles, with two currants plumped for the two eyes; place it in the middle of your difh, and pour a little red wine round it.

482. *To make* GOOSEBERRY FOOL.

Pick a quart of goofeberries, put them into a fauce-pan with water to cover them, and fet them on the fire 'till they break; then pour them into a fieve, prefs the pulp thro' into the water they were boiled in, and put it into a pan with the yolks of fix eggs beat, and half a pound of fugar, keep ftiring it 'till it's thick, then pour it into a bafon, and keep it for ufe.

483. *To make* RASPBERRY FOOL.

Take a pint of rafpberries when ripe, prefs them thro' a fieve, put to the juice, fix ounces of loaf fugar; beat the yolks of two eggs with a jill of cream; put your

juice

juice into a pan, set it over the fire, then put in your cream and egg, keeping it stirring all the time 'till it's thickened a little, pour it into a deep dish, and eat it cold. You must not let it boil.

484. *To make a* SACK POSSET.

Take a quart of cream, grate in four Naples' Biscuits, a little nutmeg, and a stick of cinnamon, and set it over the fire to boil; then take six eggs beat very well and mixed with a pint of wine, set it over a slow fire, stirring it 'till it be as thick as custard; set a deep dish over a stove, and put in your wine and eggs by degrees, when your cream is boiling hot; sweeten it to your taste; but do not let it boil after the wine is put in, tho' it must be very hot; make it a little before you use it, set it upon the hearth, and cover it 'till you serve it up.

485. *To make an* ORANGE POSSET.

Take three Sevile oranges, pare and juice them into the dish you intend to serve it in, adding to it a jack of white wine, and some sugar, stirring it 'till it be melted; then boil a pint of cream with a little sugar, and pour it into a tea-pot; set your dish on the ground and pour it in, holding your hand a great height to make it bleb; set it to cool; take your rhind, clip it with a pair of scissars long and small like straw, put it into water as you clip it, and boil it in spring water 'till tender; make syrrup of it of fine
su-

sugar, put in your peel, and boil it 'till it looks clear, drain it from the syrrup, lay it over your posset, and serve it up.

486. *To make* LEMON POSSETS.

Take a pint of cream, put in the rhinds of two, and the juice of one lemon, and a jack of white wine, sweeten it to your taste, bleb it with a spoon, and fill your glasses; if you chuse to have it in a dish, boil the rhind as above.

487. *To make* CURRANT POSSETS.

Take a pint of the juice of red currants, sweeten it with loaf sugar, and put to it a jill of cream; bleb them with a spoon, and fill your glasses, or put them into a dish.

488. *To make* SYLLABUBS.

Take a pint of cream, sweeten it, whisk it with a whisk, and lay it upon a sieve to drain; take some white and some red wine in separate basons, sweetened, fill your glasses about three parts full, and when your froth is drained, lay it on. You may make half of them white and half red.

489. *To make* WHITE LEMON CREAM.

Take a pint of spring-water, the whites of six eggs, beat them very well to a froth, and put them to your water, with half a pound of double refined sugar, a spoonful of orange flower water, and the juice of three lemons, mix all together, and strain them thro' a fine cloth into a silver tankard; set it over a slow fire in a chafingdish, and

keep

keep stirring it all the time; as you see it thicken, take it off; it will sooner curdle than be yellow, stir it till it be cold, and put it in small jelly glasses for use.

490. *To make* BLANCHTMONGE.

Take an ounce of isinglass, boil it in a pint of water till it wastes to two spoonfuls; take a quart of cream and boil it with a stick of cinnamon, some lemon peel, a little loaf sugar to your taste, eight or nine bitter almonds beat fine in a stone mortar, and boil with your cream; put it to the isinglass, and let it have a boil together; strain out the almonds and the rest from it, put it into glasses, and when you would turn it out, dip the glasses into warm water

491. *To make* YELLOW LEMON CREAM.

Take two or three lemons according as they are in bigness, peel them as thin as you can from the white, put it into a pint of water, and let it lay three or four hours; take the yolks of four eggs beat very well, put half a pound of double refined sugar into your water to dissolve, and a spoonful or two of rose-water or orange flower water, which you can get, mix all together, with the juice of two of your lemons, or if they prove not good, put in three, strain them thro' a fine cloth into a silver tankard, set all over a stove, stirring it all the time, and when it begins to be as thick as cream take it off; do not let it boil, if you do it will curdle,

curdle, stir it till cold, put it into your glasses, and it is ready for use.

492. *To make* RHENISH CREAM.

Take a pint of rhenish wine, and boil it with a stick of cinnamon; take half a pound of sugar, seven yolks of eggs, beat them with a spoonful of orange flower water, and pour your wine to them, whisk it till it be so thick that you may lift it with the point of a knife, but be sure you do not let it curdle, pour it into your dish, and when its cold, stick it with citron.

493. *To make* CHOCOLATE CREAM.

Take four ounces of chocolate, grate and boil it in a pint of cream, then mill it very well with the chocolate stick; take the yolks of two eggs, and beat them very well, leaving out the strains, mix to them a little of your cream, so put them together, and set them on the fire, stirring it till it thickens, but do not let it boil; sweeten it to your taste, and keep stirring it till it be cold; then put it into your glasses, or on a china dish, which you please.

494. *To make* APPLE CREAM.

Take six large codlings, or any other apples that will be soft, coddle them, and when they are cold, take out all the pulps; then add the whites of five eggs, leaving out the strains, three quarters of a pound of double-refined sugar, beat all together

for

for an hour 'till it be white; then lay it on a china dish, so serve it up.

495. *To make* QUINCE CREAM.

Take your quinces and coddle them 'till they are soft, bruise the clear part of them, and pulp it thro' a sieve; take an equal weight of quince and double refined sugar beat and sifted; take three whites of eggs beat to a froth, put your quince to your eggs, and beat them till they be white, then place it in the form of a pile on your dish.

496. AMBASSADOR CREAM.

Beat three whites of eggs to a froth, put to them as much currant jelly as will colour them, whisk them till stiff, then drop them off a knife point upon the dish you design for it. You may make this of the syrrup of any preserved fruit, if it be rich.

497. *To make* SHENELL.

Take six yolks of eggs boiled, put to them three ounces of butter, a quarter of a pound of loaf-sugar, beat all together in a mortar, with two spoonfuls of orange flower water, and rub it through a cullender on the plate or dish you design for it.

498. *To make* FLUMMERY.

Take a pint of stiff calf's foot jelly, a pint of cream, two ounces of bitter almonds, and two of sweet, sweeten it to your taste, and boil it; strain it thro' a cloth, and keep stirring it now and then till its cold; dip the things you design to put it in, in cold wa-

water, fill them, set them in a cool place, loosen it round the top, and it will turn out.

499. *To make* HARTSHORN FLUMMERY.

Take a pint of jelly of hartshorn very stiff, a pint of cream, two ounces of bitter, and two of sweet almonds, sweeten it to your taste, boil and strain it thro' a cloth, stir it 'till cold, wet your cups in cold water, and fill them; when you turn it, stick them with blanched almonds cut long, if you please. Your almonds must be blanched and beaten in a mortar with a little cream, before you boil them in your flummery.

500. BACON *and* EGGS.

Take a pint of flummery prepared as above, boil a little with your chocolate to make it brown, pour as much into a pot as will be the thickness of bacon swarth, and set it to cool; then have some white, cold, but not stiff, pour it upon your swarth an inch thick, set it to cool; take some more, and colour it with the red colouring, and when cold, pour it on your other, for the red to be three inches thick, then set it to cool; colour some with saffron; take six half egg shells, set them in salt, put in yellow the thickness of half the yolk of an egg, and set them to cool; dip a plate in water, pour a little flummery thin over it to be the white of your eggs, and set it to cool; when they are all cold, dip your pot in hot water, cut it in slices, and turn it out of your shells upon your plate which has your flummery on, cut the white round a little larger then the yolk, lay your sliced bacon upon the dish, and the eggs upon it.

501. *To make* Cards.

Boil three ounces of isinglass in a pint of water till its all dissolved; blanch and beat two ounces of bitter almonds, put them to it, with a pint of cream and a jill of milk, sweetened to your taste; boil and strain it thro' a cloth, and keep stirring it till its cold; dip a mazareen dish in water, pour it all over your dish the thickness of a card, and set it to cool; take the remainder and divide it in two, boil a little chocolate in one, and a little red colouring in the other, when it is cold, dip two plates in water, and pour one part upon one, and the other part on the other, set them to cool, take the dish and cut the white into cards; then take tins, and cut peeps out of your cards, cut peeps out of the red with the same tin, and put them into your cards the shape of diamonds and hearts; you must cut the other out with tins the shape of spades and clubs, so you may make them what cards you chuse.

502. *To make a* Nest *of* Eggs.

Take a pint of stiff calf's foot jelly, a jill of white wine, the juice of three lemons, sweeten all to your taste; beat four whites of eggs to a froth, mix all together in a pan, and boil them, strain them through a

dimi-

dimithy bag, when its clear, let it run into a bason a quarter full, and set it to cool; set another bason for it to run into, take five small eggs, break little holes in the sides, and pour out your eggs, wash the shells, fill them with flummery, and set them to cool; pare the rhinds of two lemons, and cut them with a pair of scissars to be like straw, boil it in spring water till its tender, drain it out of the water, boil it in a syrrup of double refined sugar till it be clear, and take it out to drain; take your flummery out of the shells, and put them into the bason which you set to cool, lay one in the middle and the others round, put the straw betwixt them, pour the remainder of your jelly upon them till your bason is full, and set it to cool, when cold set your bason a minute in hot water, put your plate upon your bason, and turn it out, break a little cold jelly with a spoon, and lay it rough round.

503. *To make a* MELLON.

Beat eight eggs with a spoonful of rosewater, and a pound of beaten and sifted loaf sugar, for an hour, put in a pound of flower well dried, butter your mould the shape of a mellon, fill it, and bake it in a quick oven. If there be more than will fill your mellon, put it in queen-cake tins; when baked, ice your little ones with white iceing, colour some with the juice of spinage, ice your mel-

mellon all over, and set it to dry; they are pretty in a desert.

504. *To make* CALF's-FOOT JELLIES.

To a gang of calf's-feet washed, put a gallon of water, boil them till half be wasted, strain it through a hair sieve into a bowl, set it to cool, and when its cold, take the fat clear off the top; the settling of the bottom put into a pan, with a quart of white wine, the juice of six lemons, two drops of cinnamon, the whites of eight eggs beaten to a froth, a glass of brandy, sweeten all to your taste, and set it over your fire to boil; keep stirring it all the time it boils; pour it into your bag, change your bason, and pour it into your bag till it runs clear.

505. *To make* HARTSHORN JELLIES.

Take a pound of hartshorn, put to it a gallon of spring water, let it boil gently till half be wasted, strain it, and let it stand till its cold; then put to it the juice of six lemons, a quart of white wine, a glass of brandy, the whites of eight eggs beaten to a froth, two drops of cinnamon, mix all together, boil them, and pour them into your bag, cover them to keep them warm, and they will run the quicker off.

506. *To make* RIBBON JELLY.

Take a quart of stiff jelly, a pint of white wine, the juice of three lemons, five whites of eggs beaten to a froth, sweeten it to your taste, boil it, and pour it into a bag; then run

run the jelly into high glasses, let every colour be as thick as your finger; one colour must be cold before you put another on, for fear of mixing; colour one with the red colouring; one with green; one with saffron; one with syrrup of violets; one white with pounded almonds; and one with jelly, till your glasses are full. You make make it without wine, if you chuse.

507. *To make* CRAY-FISH *in* JELLY.

Take a knuckle of veal, chop it with your clever, and boil it in a gallon of water, skimming it clean, put in a blade or two of mace, and when its reduced to three pints, strain it, and let it cool; then put it into a pan with the whites of four eggs, beaten to a froth, half a jack of madeira, a little salt, boil it, and run it thro' a jelly bag to look clear, fill a bason, the bigness of your dish you intend to serve it in, better than a quarter full, and set it to cool; have ready some cray-fish, boiled and cold; wipe them with a cloth, and lay them on their backs in the bowl upon your jelly; take your other jelly and pour it on them blood warm to cover them; when it is cold set your bowl a minute in hot water, and turn it out. You may break a little jelly with a spoon, and lay it rough round.

508. *To make* CURRANT JELLY.

Take ripe currant berries, and pick them from the stalks, one quart of white to two of red, bruise them, and strain the juice; to a pint of juice put a pint of double-refined sugar beaten fine, set it over your stove, and boil it 'till any skim will arise, then fill your glasses, and the next day clip a paper round, dip it in brandy, and lay it upon your jelly.

509. *To make a* JELLY *of* PIPPINS.

Take the fairest and firmest pippins, pare them, and put as much spring water to them as will cover them, set them over a quick fire, and boil them to mash; put them on a sieve, press the pulp through, and strain the jelly thro' a bag; to every pint of it put a pound of double refined sugar beaten, boil it 'till any skim will arise, then fill your glasses; dip paper in brandy, and lay it on your jelly the next day.

510. *To make a* JELLY *of* BULLIES.

Take what quantity of bullies you please, pick off the stalks, put them in a pot, cover the top close, and set it in boiling water 'till they are enough; strain the liquor from the bullies thro' a hair sieve; to every quart of liquor put a pound and a half of sugar, boil it over a slow fire, and keep stirring it all the time. You may know when it's boiled high enough by its parting from the pan; pour it into pots, and cover it with papers dipped in brandy, lay another paper over them, and tie them close up.

511. *To*

511. *To make a* JAM *of* BULLIES.

Take the bullies that remain in the sieve, and to every pound of them, put a pound of sugar, boil it over a slow fire, and put it into pots, with papers tied over them, and keep them for use.

512. *To make* RASPBERRY JAM.

Take a pint of raspberries, bruise them in a jill of currants juice, put in a pound and a half of loaf sugar beaten, boil it over a slow fire, stirring it all the time 'till it will jelly; then pour it into your pots, put on papers dipped in brandy, and tie papers over them.

513. *To preserve* RASPBERRIES.

Take the largest and fairest raspberries you can get; to every pound of berries, put a pound and a half of double refined sugar beaten, put your sugar into a pan with a jill of currant juice to every pound, boil and skim it clean; then put in your raspberries, let them boil, and keep them whole; let your syrrup be so rich that it will hang in flakes upon your spoon; take them off the fire, skim them well, and put them into in your pots.

514. *To make* RASPBERRY CLEAR CAKES.

Take two quarts of white currants, and one quart of red raspberries, put them into a stone jar and stop them close, set the jar in a pot of boiling water 'till they are enough; then put them into a hair sieve set over a pan;

pan; press out all the jelly, and strain it thro' a jelly bag; to every pound of jelly, take twenty ounces of double-refined sugar, boil it over a slow fire, skim it well, and fill your clear cake glasses; then take off what skim is on them, and set them into the stove to dry; when you find them hard on the upper-side, turn them out upon squares of glass, set them in again, and when they candy, cut them in squares or what pieces you please, and let them lay 'till they are hard, then put them on sieves, and when thoroughly dry, put them in boxes. You may do white raspberries the same way.

515. *To preserve* APRICOTS *Green.*

Take apricots before the stones are hard, and that you can put a pin thro' them, rub them with a coarse wet cloth, and a little salt, 'till all the roughness is off; then put them into a pan with spring water, cover them with vine leaves, and set them over a slow fire to keep hot 'till they are green, take them out of the water, weigh them, and take their weight in double refined sugar, dip your sugar in spring water, and make your syrrup; when almost cold, wipe your apricots, put them in, and boil them 'till they look clear; put your apricots into your pots; boil your syrrup, skim it, and pour it on them; set them to cool, and cover them up.

516. *To*

516. *To preserve* APRICOTS.

Take apricots before they be full ripe, stone and pare them thin, weigh them, and take their weight in double-refined sugar; put in as much water to it as will wet it, boil your syrrup, and skim it 'till no skim arise, when it's near cold put in your apricots, and give them a boil; take them into a bowl, pour your syrrup over them, and lay something on them to keep them in the syrrup 'till the next day, then put them into a pan, boil them 'till they look clear, and put them into your pots; boil your syrrup, 'till it's thick and clear, strain it thro' a piece of muslin, and fill your pots up with it, and when they are cold, paper them up for use: Be careful in taking the stones out to keep them whole, and let them lay in spring water 'till you make your syrrup which makes them of a paler colour. Break the stones, take out the kernels whole, and put them in cold water to take the skins off, wipe, dry, and put them into your pots with your apricots.

517. *To preserve* DAMSINS.

Take damsins before they are full ripe, wipe and pick them, take their weight in loaf sugar, and as much water as will wet it, boil and skim it, and when cold, put in your damsins, and let them have a scald; the next day scald them again, 'till they look clear, then put them into your pots; boil and skim your syrrup 'till it's thick, then strain it, fill your pots, and cover them up for use. You must not let your damsins boil.

518. *To preserve* BARBERRIES.

Take full ripe barberries, strip them from the stalks, and put to them their weight in sugar, and as much water as will wet it, boil and skim it; then put in your barberries, let them boil 'till they look clear, and your syrrup thick, then put them in pots, and when they are cold, cover them up for use.

519. *To make* BARBERRY DROPS.

Take full-ripe barberries, strip them off the stalks, cover them up in a pot, and set it in a pan of boiling water 'till they are soft, and pulp them through a hair sieve; take as much searsed sugar mixed with the pulp as will make it into a light paste, then drop them with a pen knife on paper, glazed with a smooth stone, and set them within the air of the fire to dry; when they are dry, put them into a box, and keep them in a dry place.

520. *To preserve* ORANGES.

Take six clear Sevile oranges, the largest you can get, scrape the rhind with a penknife, put them in spring water, and let them lay twenty-four hours, changing the water; cut a round bit out of the stalk end, and scoup the meat out with a little spoon, tie them in cloths, and boil them in spring water,

sup-

supplying them with boiling water as it wastes away; take six pounds of double-refined sugar, and as much water as will wet it, boil and skim it, when your oranges are tender, take them out of the cloths, put them into the syrrup, and let them have a boil, then stand twenty-four hours; then boil them 'till they look clear, and put them into a pot; boil your syrrup 'till it's thick, and pour it upon them, and when they are cold put on a paper dipped in brandy, and tie another paper over, take the skins and pippins out of the pulp, put to it half a pound of sugar, and boil it.

521. *To preserve* QUINCES.

Take the largest full grown quinces, pare them, put them into water, cut them in quarters, and take out the cores, (if you would have any whole, you must take out the cores with a scoup,) take their weight in sugar with as much water as will make a syrrup, boil and skim it, put in your quinces and parings when it is cold; set them over a slow fire, covered with syrrup, pound a bit of cochineal, tie it in a rag, put it into your pan, and press it to the side with a spoon 'till your quinces look red; let them boil 'till they look clear, and the syrrup thick, put them in a pot, strain your syrrup thro' a piece of muslin, and when cold lay on a paper dipped in brandy, and tie another paper over them.

522. *To make* Quinces *White.*

Pare your quinces, put them in water, and coddle them 'till they are tender; to every pound of quince, put a pound of loaf sugar, boil your syrrup skim it very well, put your quinces into it; and boil them 'till they look clear, and when cold, cover them close up.

523. *To preserve* Green Figs.

Take green figs, nick them on the tops, put them in salt and water ten days; make your pickle as follows,—put in as much salt into the water as will make it bear an egg, put in your figs, cover them with vine leaves and hang them over a flow fire, 'till they are green, then drain them, and put them into fresh warm water, shifting them four times in two days, weigh them, and to every pound of figs, put a pound of double refined sugar, and as much water as will wet it, boil and skim it, and put in your figs, well drained, scald them, and let them stand 'till the next day, then boil them till they look clear, and your syrrup thick, strain your syrrup, and put them up for use.

524. *To preserve* Ripe Figs.

Take the white figs when ripe, nick them in the tops, take their weight in fine sugar, and give them a good boil; the next day boil them again, take them up, and put them into the pot you design to keep them in; boil and skim your syrrup, and strain it over them.

525. *To preserve* WINE SOURS.

Take your wine sours, wipe, prick and weigh them; take their weight in fine sugar, dip your sugar in water, and make it into a syrrup, skim it, and when it is near cold, pour it over your plumbs; let them stand 'till the next day, and give them a gentle heat; let them stand a day longer, then heat them again, take the plumbs out, and drain them; boil the syrrup, and skim it well; then put the syrrup on the wine sours, and when cold, put them into pots; if the skin slips, you may close them with your fingers, tie a bladder close over the top, and keep them for use.

526. *To preserve* WHITE PEAR PLUMBS.

Take the fairest pear plumbs you can get without spots, gathered when they are almost ripe, let them stand a day and a night before you preserve them; wipe them with a linen cloth, and cut the skins down the seams with a sharp knife, cut away a little of the stalks, and to two pounds of plumbs put two pounds and a half of fine loaf sugar; clarify your sugar with the whites of two eggs; take as much water as will cover your plumbs, let the syrrup boil quick, and strain it into the pan you preserve in, boil and skim it clean, then lay in your plumbs one by one with the seams downwards, set them on a slow fire, and keep them in the hot syrrup 'till the skins break;

turn them, and let them lay half a quarter of an hour in the syrrup without boiling; then make a quick fire, let them boil up, and as the skins rise, take them off, and skim them; then set them on again, and continue doing so 'till you see the syrrup thick, clear and white; then take them up into a silver dish one by one, and as you take them out of the pan, close the seams with a silver bodkin, and when they are almost cold, put them into glasses; if your syrrup do not jelly, let it boil again, pour now and then a ladle full on them 'till it's hot, and keep the rest 'till it is cold to cover them.

527. *To preserve* MORELLA CHERRIES.

Take your cherries, wipe them, wash the stalks, and cut a little off the ends; to every pound of cherries put a pound of double refined sugar, wet with a pint of white currant juice, and a glass of brandy; you must allow a pound of sugar for a pint of juice, so make your syrrup, and skim it; then put in your cherries, and when they have had a heat, take them up into a bowl; boil the syrrup and pour it on them; do so three times, and when your cherries are enough, boil the syrrup up higher, strain it on them, and when they are cold, put them in pots, cover them with a paper dipped in brandy, and tie them up close.

528. *To dry* CHERRIES.

To every five pounds of cherries stoned, put

put a pound of double refined sugar; put the sugar first into your pan with a very little water, then your cherries, make them scalding hot, then take them immediately out of the syrrup, and dry them; put them into the pan again, strewing pounded sugar between every layer of cherries, set them on the fire, and make them scalding hot as before; which must be done twice with the sugar; then drain them from this syrrup, and lay them singly to dry in the sun, or in a stove; when they are dry, throw them into a bason of cold water, but take them out again the same moment, dry them with a cloth, and set them into the hot sun or stove, and keep them in a dry place. This is not only the best way to give them a good taste, but for colour and plumpness.

529. *To preserve Yellow* AMBER PLUMBS.

Take your plumbs, wipe and prick them, to every pound of plumbs put a pound of double refined sugar, dipped in water to make a syrrup, put in your plumbs, let them have a scald; the next day, boil them slow till they look clear, put your plumbs into your pots, boil your syrrup, strain it, and pour it on; and when they are cold, cover them up for use.

530. *To preserve* GRAPES.

Take the largest and best grapes before they are ripe, scald them in a thin syrrup two or three days, then put them into clarified

rified sugar, give them a good boil, and skim them; put them into our pots, strain your syrrup over them, and when cold, cover them for use.

531. *To preserve* GOOSEBERRIES.

To a pound of stoned gooseberries, put a pound of double refined sugar, dip your sugar in water, and make a syrrup of it; then put in your gooseberries, and boil them till they be clear, and your syrrup thick, put them into pots, and cover them up.

532. *To preserve* RED GOOSEBERRIES.

Take three pounds of sugar, and a gill of currant juice, and make a syrrup of it; have ready picked four pounds of red gooseberries, put them into your syrrup, and let them boil slowly for a quarter of an hour, to keep them whole, put them in your pots for use, and cover them.

533. *To preserve* MEDLARS.

Scald your fruit in spring water, till the skins may be easily peeled off, then stone them at the head, adding to every pound of medlars a pound of sugar, let them boil till the liquor becomes ropy, then take them off the fire, and keep them for use.

534. PEACHES *in* BRANDY.

Put your peaches into boiling water, but do not let them boil; take them out, put them in cold water, then drain them, and put them in wide mouthed bottles; to six peaches, take half a pound of loaf sugar clarified,

clarified, put it over your peaches, fill up the bottles with good brandy, stop them close, and keep them in a cool place.

535. *To preserve* LEMONS.

Cut a round bit out of the stalk end of your lemons, and scoop the meat out, put them into spring water, and let them lay twenty-four hours, changing the water; then tie them up in cloths, and boil them in spring water till tender; to every lemon put a pound of double refined sugar, and as much water to it as will wet it and make a syrrup; then take your lemons out of the cloths, drain them, put them into your syrrup, and let them boil; the next day boil them till they look clear, put them into your pots, let your syrrup have a boil, and pour it on them, and when cold, cover them close with paper dipped in brandy.

536. *To candy* ANGELICA.

Boil the stalks of angelica in water 'till they are tender, then peel them, put them in warm water, and cover them, till they are very green, over a gentle fire, lay them on a cloth to dry; take their weight in fine sugar, and boil it to a candy height with a little rose water, then put in your stalks, boil them up quick, and take them out in order to be dried for use.

537. *To candy* GINGER.

Take the fairest pieces, pare off the rhind, and lay them in water twenty-four hours;
then

then boil double refined sugar to a candy height, and when almost cold, put in your ginger, and stir it till its hard to the pan; then take it out piece by piece, lay it near the fire, and then put it into a warm pan, tie it up close, and the candy will be firm.

538. *To candy* ALMONDS.

Blanch your almonds, throw them into sugar boiled to a candy height, and let them all together have a warm, keeping your almonds stirring to the end, that the sugar may stick close to them, take them out, and lay them to dry.

539. *To candy* ORANGE CHIPS.

Pare your oranges not over thin, but narrow, throw them into water as you pare them off, boil them till tender; then make a syrrup of loaf sugar, boiled to a candy height, put your peels in, let them boil, and let them lay in the syrrup two or three days; then boil them again, take them out and lay them on a sieve to drain with the rhind upper-most, then dry them by the fire or in a stove.

540. *To make* BARLEY SUGAR.

Boil a sufficient quantity of barley in water, strain it thro' a hair sieve, and let this decoction be put into clarified sugar brought to the caramel, or last degree of boiling; then take the pan off the fire 'till the boiling settles, and pour your barley sugar upon a marble stone rubbed with oil, and as

it

it cools and begins to grow hard, cut it into pieces, and roll it in what lengths you pleafe.

541. *To know when* SUGAR *is at Candy-height.*

Take fome double-refined fugar, dip it in water, and clarify it 'till it comes to a candy-height, ftir it with a ftick, and when it is at candy height, it will fly from your ftick like flakes of fnow, and 'till it comes to that height, it will not fly. You may ufe it as you pleafe.

542. *To preferve* GOLDEN PIPPINS.

Take a pound of clear found pippins, pare them, take out the eyes, and throw them into fpring water; take a pound of double refined fugar, a pint of fpring water, fet it on the fire, and put your pippins into it, and let them boil eight minutes; then take them off to cool a little, and fet them on again, and let them boil as long as they did before; do this three or four times, 'till they look very clear; then take the rhinds of two lemons, clip them like ftraw, and boil them 'till they are tender; boil up a fyrrup 'till it looks clear, putting in a fpoonful of lemon juice; take your apples up to drain, lay them upon your difh, pour on your fyrrup, and lay your peel over them.

543. *To preferve* CODLINGS.

Put your codlings in a pan of water, and fet them over a gentle fire, cover'd clofe with vine leaves, but do not let them boil; as they are doing, turn them, and when they

they are tender, peel off the skins; put them into your pan again, and cover them with leaves 'till they look green; make a syrrup of fine sugar, and when cold, drain your codlings, put them in, and let them have a scald; then take them out, put them into pots, boil your syrrup, and pour it over them.

544. *To make* BLACK CAPS.

Take six large apples, scoup out all the cores, place them on a dish with their skins on, grate a little sugar on them, and set them in a hot oven 'till the skins are a little black, and the apples tender; when enough lay them on a dish, put a little raspberry jam in the middle of the apples, and grate some more sugar over them; have ready two ounces of rice creed and drained, put to it a glass of white wine, a stick of cinnamon, and three spoonfuls of cream, sweeten it to your taste, and set it upon the fire 'till it be stiff, then lay it in heaps with your apples, and serve them up hot.

545. *To make* SYRRUP *of* LEMONS.

To a pint of juice put a pound and half of double refined sugar, simmer it to a syrrup over a slow fire, stirring it often, after its settled from the dregs, pour off the syrrup, and keep it in bottles for use.

546. *To make* SHRUB.

Take five gallons of brandy, five quarts of orange juice, four pounds of double refined

fined sugar, mix'd all well together, till the sugar is diſſolved, put it in a caſk, let it ſtand till its fine, then draw it off.

547. *To make* Syrrup *of* Mulberries.

Take mulberries when they are full ripe, break them well with your hand, and drop them thro' a bag; to every pound of juice, put a pound of loaf-ſugar beaten fine, put it to your juice, boil and ſkim it well all the time its boiling; when the ſkim hath done riſing its enough, and when cold, bottle, and keep it for uſe.

548. *To make* Syrrup *of* Cowslips.

Take a quartern of freſh pick'd cowſlips, put to them a quart of boiling water, and let them ſtand all night; the next morning drain it from the cowſlips; to every pint of water put a pound of loaf ſugar, boil it over a ſlow fire, ſkim it all the time its boiling, while no ſkim riſes, then take it off, and when cold, put it into a bottle, and keep it for uſe.

549. *To make* Lemon Brandy.

To a gallon of brandy, put five quarts of water, two dozen of lemons, two pounds of the beſt ſugar, and three pints of milk; pare your lemons very thin, lay the peels in the brandy to ſteep twelve hours, and ſqueeze your lemons upon the ſugar; then put water to it, and mix all your ingredients together; boil your milk and pour it in boiling, let it ſtand twenty-four hours; then

then strain it thro' a jelly bag, and if its not fine the first time, strain it till it is fine.

550. *To make* Black Cherry Brandy.

Take a gallon of the best brandy, put in eight pounds of black cherries stoned, bruise the stones in a mortar, and put them into the brandy, cover it close, let them steep a month, drain it off, and bottle it.

551. *To make* Ratifie.

Take a quart of the best brandy, and a gill of apricot kernels, blanch and bruise them in a mortar with a spoonful of brandy, put them into a bottle with your brandy, with a quarter of a pound of loaf sugar, let it stand till it has got the taste of the kernels, then pour it out into a bottle, and cork it close. You may put more brandy to your kernels, if you chuse.

552. *To make* Lemonade.

Scrape the rhind of a lemon, and juice of two, into a quart of spring water, three spoonfuls of capalare, and sweeten it to your taste.

553. *To make* Syrrup of Violets.

Take violets and pick them, to every pound of violets put a pint of water, when your water boils put it to your violets, stir them well together, let them infuse twenty-four hours, and strain them; to every pound of juice put a pound and three quarters of loaf sugar beaten, stir it 'till the sugar is dissolved, let it stand two days, stirring it three

three times a day; then set it on the fire to warm, and it will be thick enough.

554. *To make* ORGEAT.

Take two ounces of mellon seeds, half an ounce of pompion seeds, half an ounce of Jordan almonds blanched, with a quarter of an ounce of bitter almonds, beat them all in a mortar to a paste, so as to leave no lumps, sprinkling it now and then with orange flower water, to hinder it from turning to oil; when your seeds and almonds are thoroughly stamped, put in half a pound of sugar, which is to be pounded with your paste; put the paste into two quarts of water, and let it steep; then put in a spoonful of orange flower water, and pass the liquor through a straining bag, pressing the gross substance very hard, so as nothing may be left therein, put into it a glass of new milk, put your liquor into bottles, and set them in a cool place.

555. *To make a* PASTE *to wash your Hand with.*

Take a pound of blanched bitter almonds, and beat them very fine in a mortar, with four ounces of figs, when it comes to a paste, put it into a gally pot, and keep it for use. A little at a time will serve.

556. *To make* ORANGE WINE.

Take ten gallons of water, and twenty pounds of sugar, boil it half an hour, skimming all the time; have ready the peels of an hundred oranges in a tub, so thin pared that no white does appear; then pour on your boiling liquor, and keep it close; you must use none of the skins or seeds, but pick the meat clean out, and when the liquor is blood warm, put it in, with six spoonfuls of new yeast; let it work two days, then put it into a vessel, with a gallon of white wine, and a quart of brandy; let it stand a month, then bottle it, putting a lump of sugar into every bottle.

557. *To make* COWSLIP WINE.

Take thirty gallons of water and sixty pounds of sugar, boil them together three quarters of an hour, skimming it very well, then put it into a tub and let it stand 'till it be cold; then put in eighteen pecks of cowslips, two dozen of lemons pared very thin, and put the skins into the liquor; then squeeze the juice very well out of the lemons, put to it a gill of new yeast, and put it into your liquor; let it be beaten in three times a day for three days together, then tun it into a barrel cowslips and all; when it hath done working, bung it up close for three weeks, then bottle it; be sure to put good weight of sugar to it.

558. *To make* GOOSEBERRY WINE.

Take your gooseberries before they be over ripe, bruise them in a wood bowl, but not too small, lest you bruise the seeds; then measure them, and to every gallon of bruised berries, put two gallons of cold water, stir them

them well together, and let them stand a night and a day close covered; then draw your liquor from your berries into a tub; if it comes thick, you may strain it thro' a bag; to every gallon of liquor, put two pounds of loaf sugar dissolved, stir it well together, then put it into a barrel, and let it work two days; then bung it up for a week, and draw it out of the barrel thro' a bag; put the dregs out of the barrel, and wash it out with a little of the liquor, and to every gallon of liquor add half a pound more sugar, stir it well together, and put it into the same barrel again, bung it up for a month, then it will be fit for bottling.

559. *To make* CURRANTBERRY WINE.

Gather your currants full ripe, strip and bruise them, and to every gallon of the pulp, put two quarts of water, let it stand in a tub twenty-four hours, then run it thro' a hair sieve, and to every gallon of liquor, put two pounds of fine sugar, stir it till it be well dissolved, then put it into a clean barrel, let it stand two days, then draw it clear off, and put in half a pound more sugar to every gallon, stirred in well to dissolve it, wash your barrel, bung it up as close as you can, and let it stand six weeks, then bottle it; put a little sugar in every bottle. When you bruise the berries, take care that you do not bruise the seeds.

560. *To*

560. To make RAISIN WINE.

To every gallon of water, put five pounds of Malaga or Belvedere raisins, picked from the stalks and pulled in two, let them steep a fortnight, stirring them every day; then pour off the liquor, and squeeze the juice out of the raisins; put the liquor into a barrel which will just hold it, for it must be quite full, and let it stand open 'till the wine hath done hissing or making the least noise, then add a pint of French brandy to every two gallons, and stop it up close; let it stand six months before you bottle it, and do not draw it out too near the bottom of your barrel. January, February, or March are the best times to make it in, because the fruit is new.

561. To make BIRCH WINE.

To every gallon of birch water, put two pounds of loaf sugar, boil and skim it, and when it's cold put on a little yeast, and let it work a night and a day in the tub; smoak your barrel with brimstone before you put it in; put a little isinglass into a pot with a little of the wine, and let it stand within the air of the fire all night; take the whites of two eggs, beat them, and put them into the barrel with your isinglass, stir it about, bung it up, and let it stand two months before you bottle it.

562. To make ELDER WINE.

Gather elder berries ripe and dry, pick and

and bruife them with your hands, and ftrain them; then fet the liquor in earthen veffels a day to fettle, and to every quart of juice put three pints of water, and to every gallon of this liquor put three pounds of fugar; fet it in a kettle over the fire, and when it is at boiling, clarify it with the whites of four eggs, let it boil an hour, and when it's almoft cold, work it with ale yeaft; then tun it, and fill the veffel with the fame liquor as it works out; if the veffel holds about eight gallons, the wine will be fine in a month's time, and fit to bottle; and it will be fit to drink in two months. You may add to every gallon a pint of mountain wine.

563. *To make* CHERRY WINE.

Pull the ftalks, bruife the cherries, without breaking the ftones, prefs them hard thro' a hair bag, and to every gallon of liquor, put two pounds of fugar; fill your veffel, and let it work as long as it makes a noife, then ftop it up for fix weeks, and when fine, draw it off into dry bottles, putting a lump of fugar into every bottle; it will be fit to drink in three months.

564. *To make* BALM WINE.

Take a ftrike of balm leaves, put them in a tub, and pour eight gallons of fcalding hot water upon them, let it ftand all night, then run it thro' a hair fieve, and put to every gallon of liquor, two pounds of loaf-fugar, ftir it very well 'till the fugar is dif-
folved,

solved, put it into a pan, with the whites of four eggs beaten, when the skim begins to arise, take it off, let it boil half an hour, and keep skimming it all the time; then put it into the tub, and when cold, put a little new yeast upon it, and beat it in every two hours, so work it for two days; then put it into a barrel, bunged up close, and when fine, bottle it.

565. *To make* White Currant Wine.

Take your currants when they are full ripe, strip and break them with your hands till you break all the berries, and to every quart of pulp, put a quart of water, mix them well together, and let them stand all night in your tub; then strain them thro' a hair sieve, and to every gallon of liquor, put two pounds and a half of double refined sugar; when your sugar is dissolved, put it into your barrel, dissolve a little isinglass, and put it in; to every four gallons, put in a quart of mountain wine, then bung up your barrel, and when fine, draw it off, and wash out your barrel with a little of your wine, and drop the grounds thro' a bag; then put it to the rest of your wine, and put it all into your barrel again; to every gallon put half a pound more sugar; let it stand a month, then bottle it.

566. *To make* Apricot Wine.

Take twelve pounds of apricots when near ripe, wipe them clean, and cut them

in

in pieces; put to them two gallons of water, and let them boil till the liquor is strong of the apricot flavour; then strain the liquor thro' a hair sieve, and put to every quart of liquor, six ounces of fine sugar, boil it again, skim it, and when the skim hath done rising, pour it into an earthen pot; the next day bottle it, putting a lump of sugar into every bottle.

567. *To make* SAGE WINE.

Boil six gallons of spring water a quarter of an hour, and let it stand till its blood warm, put in twenty-four pounds of malaga raisins, picked and shread, with a strike of red sage shread, and a gill of ale yeast, stir all well together, and let it stand in a tub covered six days, stirring it once a day; then strain it off, put it in a small barrel, and let it work three days; then stop it up, and when it hath stood six days, put in a quart of canary; when its fine, bottle it.

568. *To make* DAMSIN WINE.

To four gallons of water, put sixteen pounds of malaga rasins, and half a peck of damsins into a tub, cover it, and let it stand six days, stir them twice every day, then draw off your wine; colour it with the juice of damsins sweetened with sugar; tun it into a wine vessel for a fortnight bunged up, then bottle it.

569. *To make* Quince Wine.

Take twenty large quinces gathered when dry, wipe them clean with a coarse cloth, then grate them as near the core as you can, but do not grate in any of the core; then boil a gallon of spring water, and put your grated quinces to it, let it boil gently a quarter of an hour; then strain the liquor into an earthen pot; and to every gallon of liquor put two pounds of fine loaf sugar, stir it till your sugar is dissolved, cover it close, and let it stand twenty-four hours, then bottle it; take care none of the sediment goes into the bottles. Your quinces must be full ripe.

570. *To make* Mulberry Wine.

Gather your mulberries when they are full ripe, and beat them in a marble mortar; to every quart of berries, put a quart of water; when you put them into the tub, mix them very well, and let them stand all night; then strain them thro' a sieve, and to every gallon of liquor, put three pounds of sugar, when your sugar is dissolved, put it into your barrel; take two pennyworth of isinglass, pulled in pieces, dissolve it in a little of the wine, put it into your barrel, and stir it about. You must not let it be over full, nor bung it too close up at first; set it in a cool place, and bottle it when fine.

571. *To make* Blackberry Wine.

Take blackberries when they are full ripe, bruise

bruise them, and put to every quart of berries, a quart of water, mix them well, and let them stand all night; then strain them thro' a sieve, and to every gallon of liquor, put two pounds and a half of sugar; when your sugar is dissolved, put it into your barrel, infusing in a little isinglass, stir it about, bung it up for six weeks, and then bottle it.

572. *To make* ELDER FLOWER WINE.

To twelve gallons of water, put thirty pounds of loaf sugar, boil it half an hour, skim it well all the time, let it stand till near cold, then put in three spoonfuls of yeast, when it works, put in two quarts of blossoms, picked from the stalks, stir it every day till it hath done working, then strain it, and put it into a vessel, bung it close, let it stand two months, then bottle it.

573. *To make* GILLIFLOWER WINE.

To three gallons of water, put six pounds of loaf sugar, boil the sugar and water together half an hour, skim it as the skim arises, and let it stand to cool; beat up three ounces of syrrup of betony, with two spoonfuls of ale yeast, mix it well together, then take a peck of gilliflowers, cut from the stalks, put them into the liquor, let them work three days covered with a cloth, strain it, and put it into a cask for a month, then bottle it.

574. *To make* STRONG MEAD.

Take six gallons of water, four pounds

of sugar, a quart of honey, two rases of ginger, a sprig of sweet-briar, and the whites of four eggs beat, mix all well together in a pan, and boil them half an hour, skimming it all the time; then put it into a tub, and when blood warm, put to it two spoonfuls of new yeast, the juice and rhinds of five lemons; let it stand three days, then put it into a barrel fit for it, bung it up, and in ten days you may bottle it.

575. *To make* SMALL MEAD.

Take six gallons of spring water, and when its hot, dissolve into it six quarts of honey, and two pounds of loaf sugar; boil it half an hour, skimming it all the time, pour it into a stand, and squeeze in the juice of eight lemons and four rhinds, four rases of ginger, and a sprig of sweet-briar; when its almost cold, put in a gill of ale yeast; put it into a cask ten days, bunged up, then bottle it.

576. *To make* SURFEIT WATER.

Take a peck of poppies well picked from the seeds, put to them half a gallon of the best annifeed water, a gallon of brandy, a pound of raisins of the sun stoned, cinnamon, cloves, mace, ginger, and nutmeg, of each a quarter of an ounce, beat them fine in a mortar, and put them to the liquor in an earthen pot, stir them all well together, and let them stand four days close covered; stir them twice a day, then strain it thro' a flannel, and bottle it.

577. *To make* BARBADOES WATER.

Pare your cittrons thin, and dry the peels in the sun, then grate the white part till you come to the pulp, put the grated into a cold still, and distil as much of that simple water as you can draw off good, with a quick fire; in the mean time, put a pound of the dried peels into a quart of the best brandy, when they are soaked enough, put to every quart of that liquor a quart of medeira wine, then distill the brandy, wine, and peels in a cold still, and put a pint of the simple water to a quart of the strong water; make syrrup of double refined sugar, to every pound of sugar, put three pints of water, and the whites of three eggs beaten; let it boil, then pass it thro' a jelly bag, 'till its very fine; put a jill of this syrrup to every quart of the mixed water, and to every quart, put a bit of allum as big as a pea; when its clear, rack it off into bottles, and put into every bottle some of the cittron flowers.

578. *To make* PLAGUE WATER.

Take rue, rosemary, balm, carduus, scordium, marrygold flowers, dragons, goats rue, mint, of each three handfuls; roots of master wort, angelica, butterbur, and pioney, of each six ounces; scorzonera, three ounces, proof spirits, three gallons; macerate, distill and make it up high proof.

579. *To make* TAR WATER.

Pour a gallon of cold water on a quart of tar, mix them very well with a stick, and let it stand forty-eight hours, for the tar to sink to the bottom; then pour off the clear water, and keep it in bottles well corked for use. Take a jill morning and night, fasting two hours both before and after, holding the nostrils till you drink, and it will not be offensive.

580. *To make* CYDER.

Take pippins, or any other apples that are of a watery juice, when they are ripe, press or pound them, and squeeze them in a hair bag, put the juice up in a cask, seasoned with a rag dipped in brimstone tied to the end of a stick put burning into the bung-hole, and when the smoak is gone, wash it with a little warm liquor that has run thro' a second straining of the murk or husk of the apples.

581. *To make* PERRY.

Take pears of a vinous juice, such as the gooseberry pear, horse-pear, the red and white, the john, the choke pear, and other pears of the like kind, the reddest of the sort, let them be ripe, grind them as you do apples for cyder, and work it off in the same manner. If your pears are of a sweet taste, mix a few crabs with them.

582. *To*

582. *To make* VERJUICE.

Having got crabs as soon as the kernels turn black, lay them on a heap to sweat, then pick them from the stalks and rottenness; stamp them to mash in a long trough with stamping beetles; make a bag of coarse hair-cloth, as square as the press, fill it with the stamped crabs, and being well pressed, put the liquor up in a clean vessel.

583. *To make different Sorts of* TARTS.

If you bake in tin patties, you must butter them, and put a little crust all over, because of taking them out; if in china or glass, no crust but the top one; lay fine sugar at the bottom, then your plumbs, cherries, or any other sort of fruit, and sugar at top, then put on your lid, and bake them in a slow oven. Minced pies must be baked in tin patties, because of the taking them out, and puff-paste is best for them. For all sweet tarts the beaten crust is the best; but do as you please. As to preserved tarts, only lay in your preserved fruit, put a very thin crust at the top, and let them be baked as little as possible; but if you would make them nice, have a large patty, the size you would have your tart, make a sugar crust, and roll it as thin as a half-penny, butter your patty, and cover it; shape your upper crust on a hollow thing on purpose, the size of your patty, and mark it with a marking iron for that purpose in what shape you pleafe, to be hollow and open that you may fee the fruit thro', then bake your cruft in a very flow oven, not to difcolour it, but to have it crifp; when the cruft is cold, very carefully take it out, fill it with what fruit you pleafe, and lay on the lid. If the tart is not eat, your fweetmeat is no worfe, and it looks genteel.

584. *Rules for* Roasting *and* Boiling Meat.

You muft put frefh meat into the water boiling hot, and your falt meat, when the water is quite cold, unlefs you think its not falted enough; for the putting it into the hot water ftrikes in the falt. Veal, lamb, and chickens, boil much whiter in a linnen cloth, with a little oat-meal or milk in the water. A leg of mutton of eight pounds weight, will take two hours boiling. A middling fized leg of lamb, an hour and a quarter. A thick piece of beef of fourteen pounds weight will take two hours and a half after the water boils; but all kinds of meat take more boiling in frofty weather; the beft rule is, to allow a quarter of an hour to every pound, half roaft all your meat for fricafeys, or elfe ftewing them too long on the fire will make them hard. When you drefs mutton or pigeons in blood, always wring in fome lemon juice to keep it from changing. When you grill any thing, let it be over a ftove of charcoal, it makes

it

it eat sweeter and shorter, turn your meat very often. When you broil fowls or pigeons, take care your fire is clear, and never baste any thing you broil, for it only makes it smoaked and burnt; mutton and pork stakes must be often turned; beef, not till one side is near done.

585. *To recover* BUTTER *when its turned to* OIL.

Take a sauce-pan with a little water and flour, and let it boil, then pour in your oily butter leisurely, stirring it at the same time.

FINIS.

A DINNER in JANUARY.
FIRST COURSE.

```
            (1)

   (2)      (3)      (4)

   (5)      (6)      (7)

   (8)      (9)     (10)

           (11)
```

1. A Pike.
2. Stewed Oysters.
3. A Boat.
4. Scotch Collops.
5. Bacon.
6. Gravy Soop.
7. Boiled Chickens.
8. Calf's Foot Pye.
9. A Boat.
10. Pork Griskins.
11. A Chine of Mutton.

SECOND COURSE.

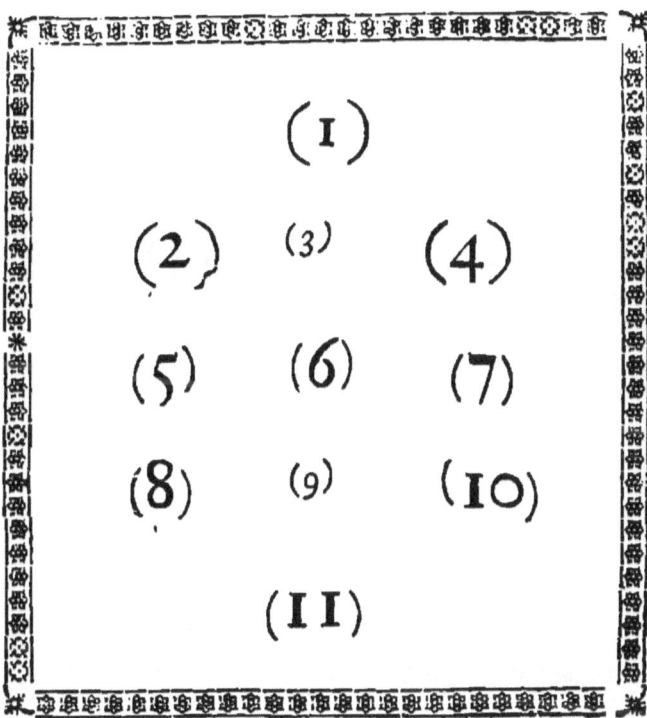

1. A Fricasey of Rabbits.
2. Oranges.
3. Apricots.
4. Cranberry Twirt.
5. Potted Hare,
6. Lemon Poffets.
7. Lobster.
8. Cheese Cakes.
9. Wine Sours.
10. Quinces.
11. Wild Ducks.

A Supper for *January*.

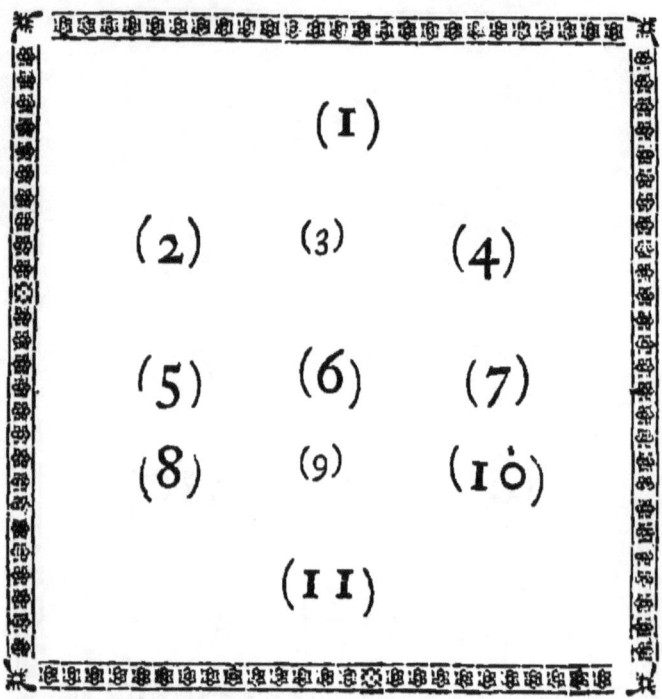

1. Boiled Fowls.
2. A Tanſey.
3. Cherries.
4. Woodcocks.
5. Calf Tongues.
6. Oranges.
7. Lobſter.
8. Apples with Rice.
9. Wine Sours.
10. Aſparagus.
11. Lamb.

A Dinner in *February*.

FIRST COURSE.

```
          (1)

  (2)    (3)      (4)

         (5)

  (6)    (7)      (8)

          (9)
```

1. Salmon and Smelts.
2. Boiled Fowls and Oyster Sauce
3. A Boat.
4. Jugged Hare.
5. Vermicelly Soop.
6. Fricasey of Pig's Feet and Ears.
7. A Boat.
8. Puddings.
9. Surloin of Beef.

SECOND COURSE.

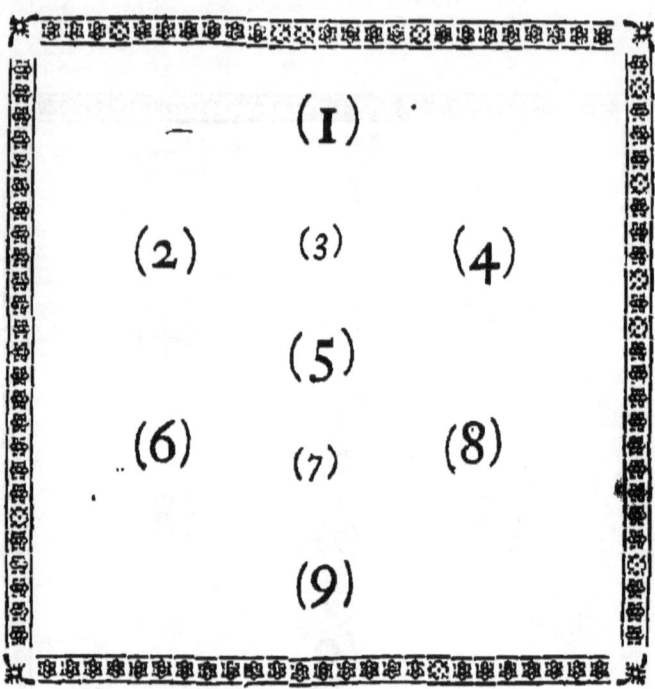

1. Sweetbreads.
2. Cuſtard.
3. Cherries.
4. Ambaſſador Cream.
5. Jellies
6. Stewed Apples.
7. Apricots green.
8. Tarts.
9. Partridges.

A Supper in *February*.

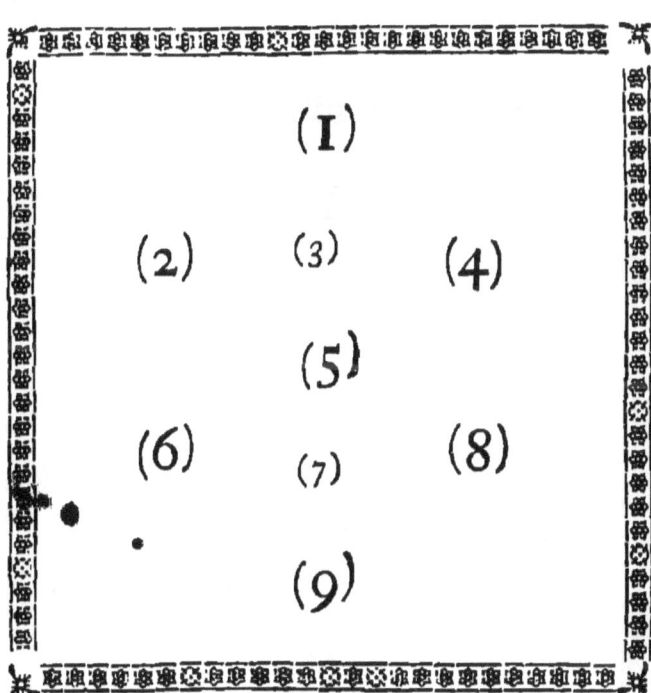

1. Scotch Collops.
2. Stewed Oysters
3. Quinces
4. Partridges
5. Syllabubs
6. Spinage and Eggs
7. Cheese Cakes
8. Minced Pies
9. Wild Ducks.

A Dinner in *March*.
FIRST COURSE.

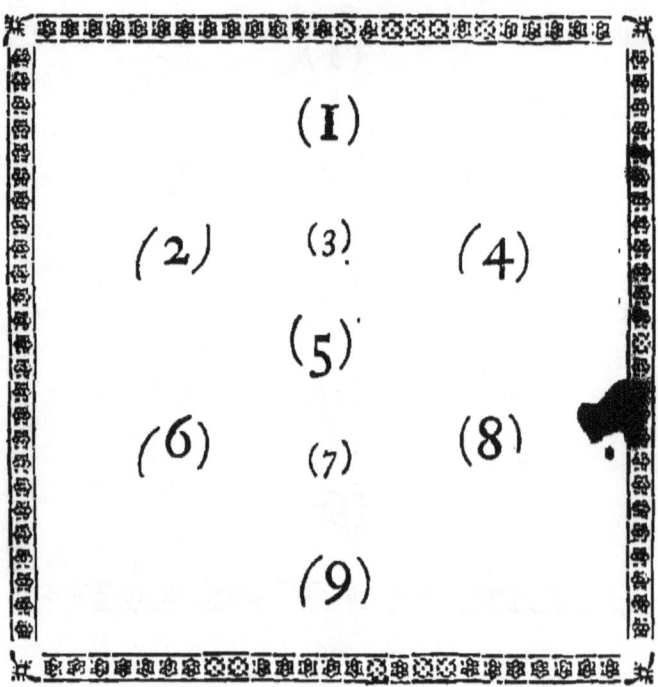

1. Stewed Tench.
2. Boiled Tongue.
3. A Boat
4. Veal A-la-dabs
5. Almond Soop.
6. Pigeon Pie
7. A Boat
8. Wild Duck.
9. Turkey Roasted.

SECOND COURSE.

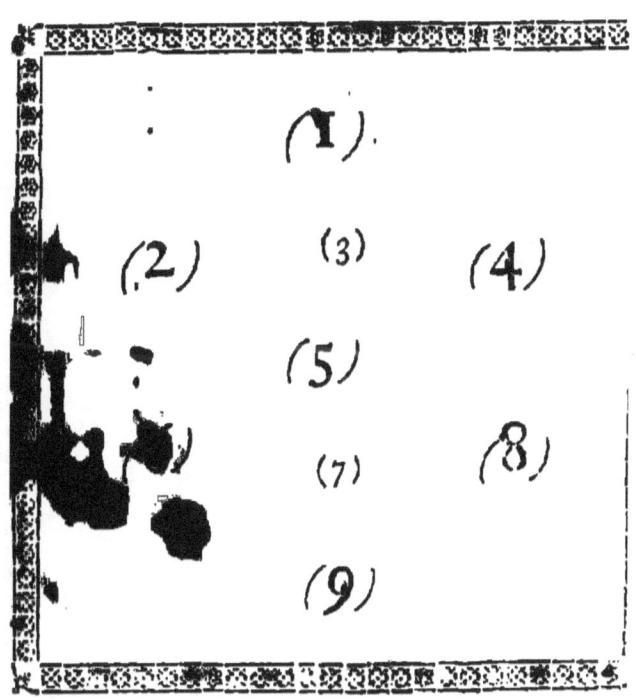

1. Woodcocks
2. Orange Poffet
3. Cheefe Cakes
4. Apricots
5. Sweetmeats
6. Wine Sours
7. Currants
8. A Trifle
9. A Roafted Pig.

A Supper in *March*.

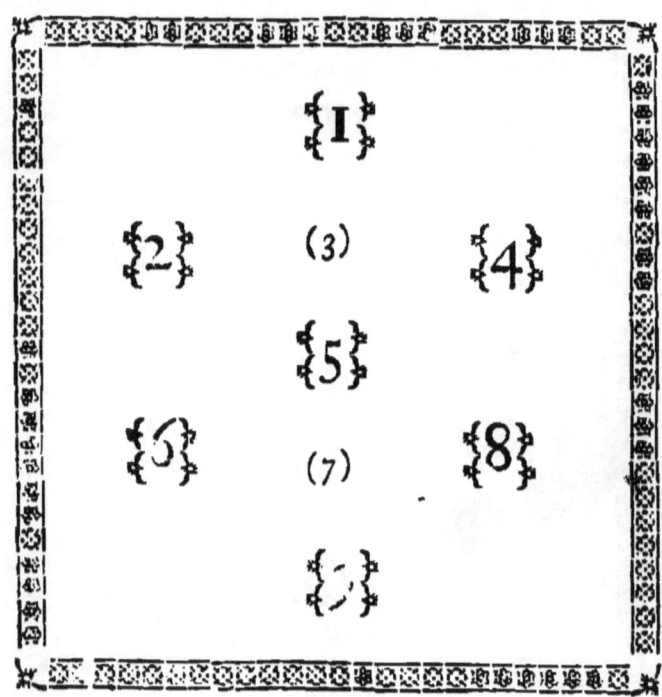

1. White Fricasey of Chickens.
2. Fritters
3. Walnuts in Sack
4. Larks
5. Jellies
6. Lamb Stakes
7. Custard
8. Buttered Crab.
9. A Capon roasted.

A Dinner in *April*.

FIRST COURSE.

```
        (1)

(2)     (3)      (4)

        (5)

(6)     (7)      (8)

        (9)
```

1. Salmon.
2. Calf's Head Haſh.
3. A Boat.
4. Hunters Pudding.
5. Muſhroom Soop.
6. Beef Stakes.
7. A Boat.
8. Stewed Pigeons.
9. A Chine of Lamb.

SECOND COURSE.

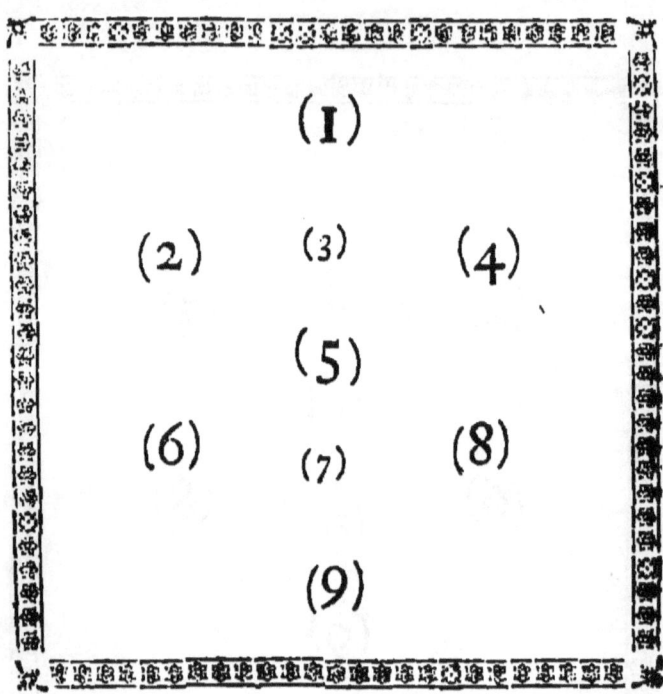

1. Roast Chickens.
2. Asparagus.
3. Rasp Cream
4. Hot Lobster.
5. Syllabubs.
6. Fricasey of Tripe.
7. Tart.
8. Artichokes.
9. Ducks.

A Supper in *April.*

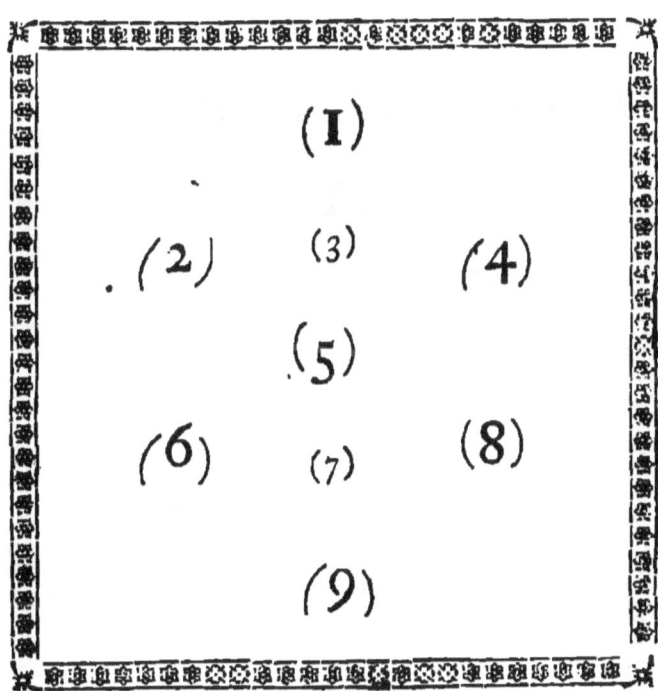

1. Veal Olives.
2. Roaſt Chickens.
3. Flummery.
4. Aſparagus.
5. Sweetmeats.
6. Goo'er Wafers
7. Curds.
8. Fried Trout.
9. A Leveret.

A Dinner in *May*.
FIRST COURSE.

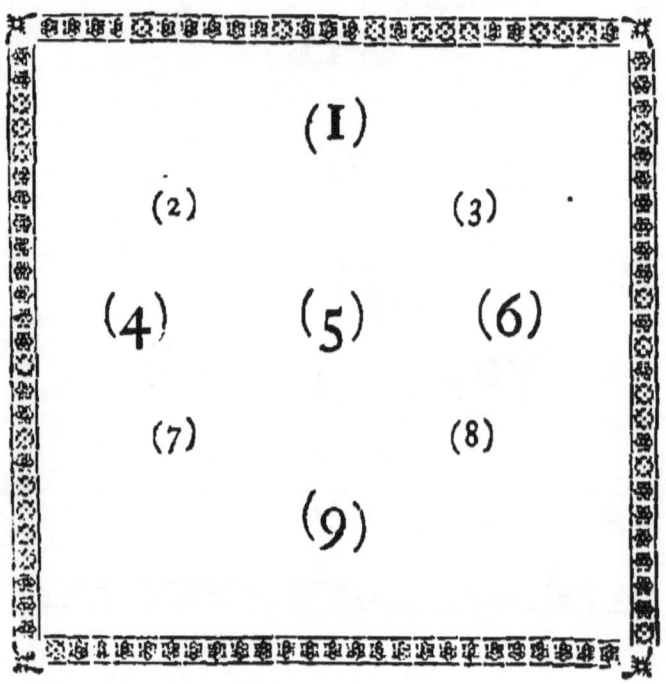

1. Breast of Veal Ragoo.
2. A Boat.
3. Beans.
4. A Goose.
5. Calf's Foot Pudding
6. Boiled Chickens.
7. Colliflower.
8. A Boat.
9. A Ham.

SECOND COURSE.

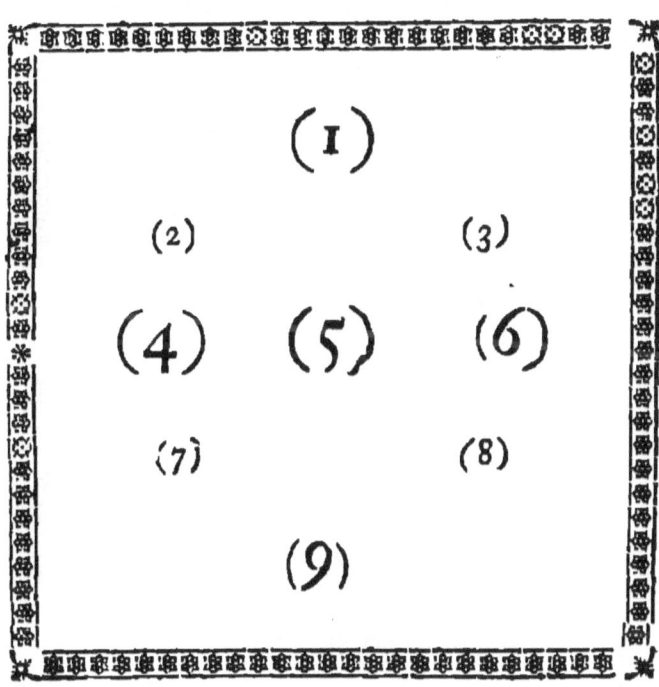

1. Pigeons and Asparagus.
2. Damsins.
3. Flummery
4. Cray Fish.
5. Preserv'd Oranges.
6. Potted Veal.
7. Curds.
8. Tart.
9. Rabbits.

A Supper for *May*.

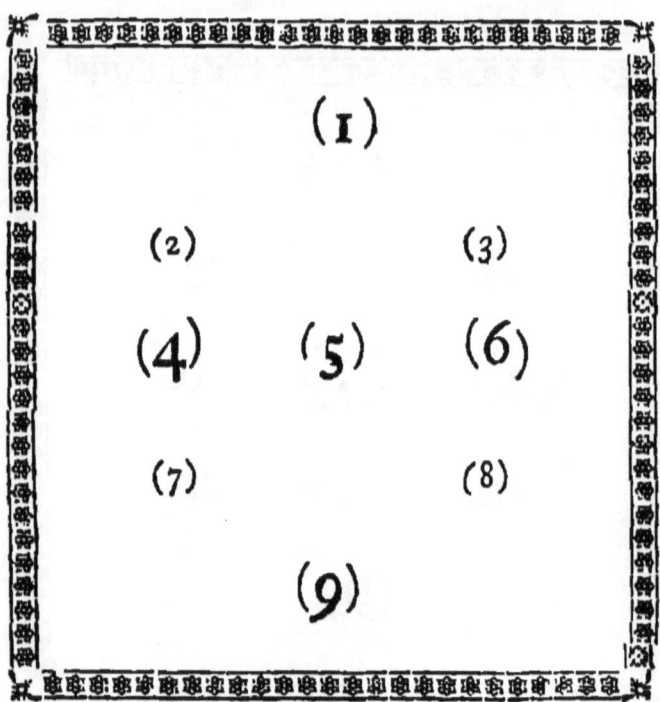

1. Lamb Fried.
2. Rhenish Cream.
3. Cherries.
4. Fried Trouts.
5. Green Apricot Tarts.
6. Asparagus.
7. Wine Sours.
8. Shenel.
9. Tame Ducks.

A Dinner in *June*.

FIRST COURSE.

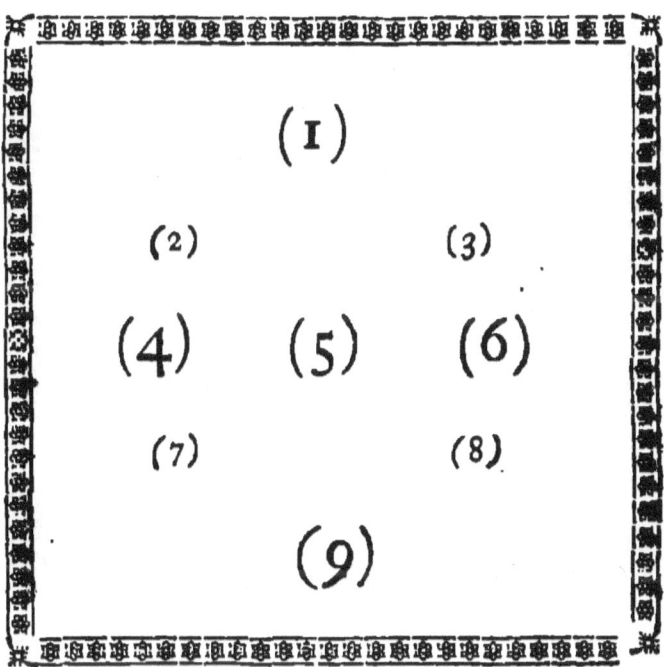

1. Mackarel.
2. Turnips.
3. Kidney Beans.
4. Veal Olives.
5. Aſparagus Soop.
6. Boiled Rabbits.
7. Colliflower.
8. Carrots.
9. A Rump of Beef.

SECOND COURSE.

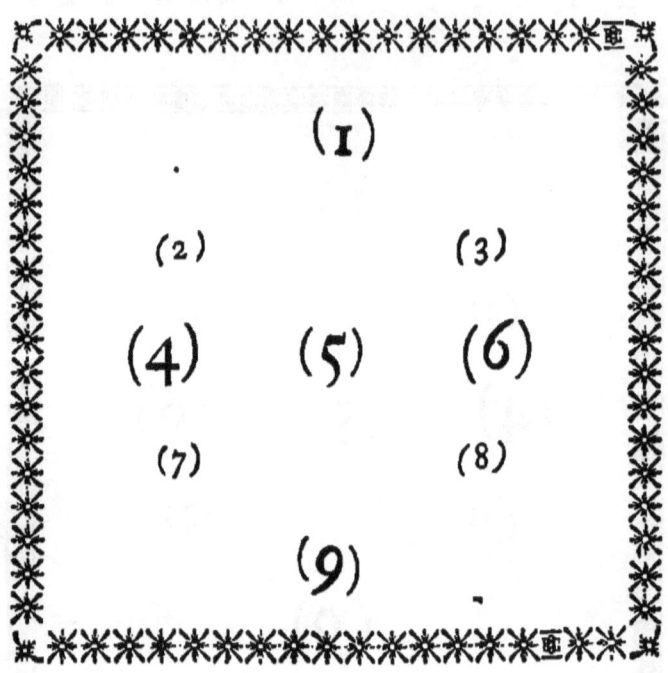

1. A Leveret.
2. Strawberries.
3. Rhenish Cream.
4. Peas.
5. Currant Poffets.
6. Artichokes.
7. Shenell.
8. Wine Sours.
9. Ducks,

A Supper in *June*.

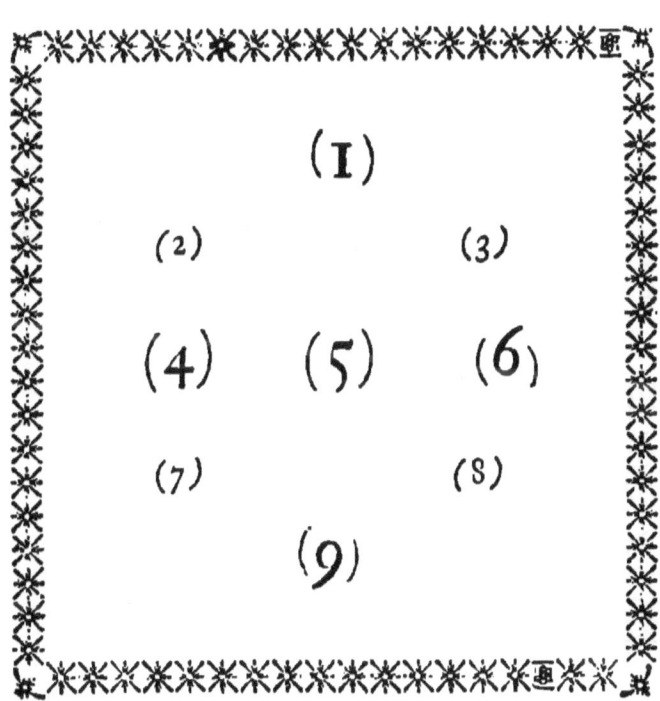

1. Veal A-la dabs.
2. Strawberries.
3. Hedge-Hog.
4. Soals.
5. Currant Poffets.
6. Sweetbreads.
7. Flummery.
8. Cherries.
9. A Neck of Venison.

A Dinner in *July*.

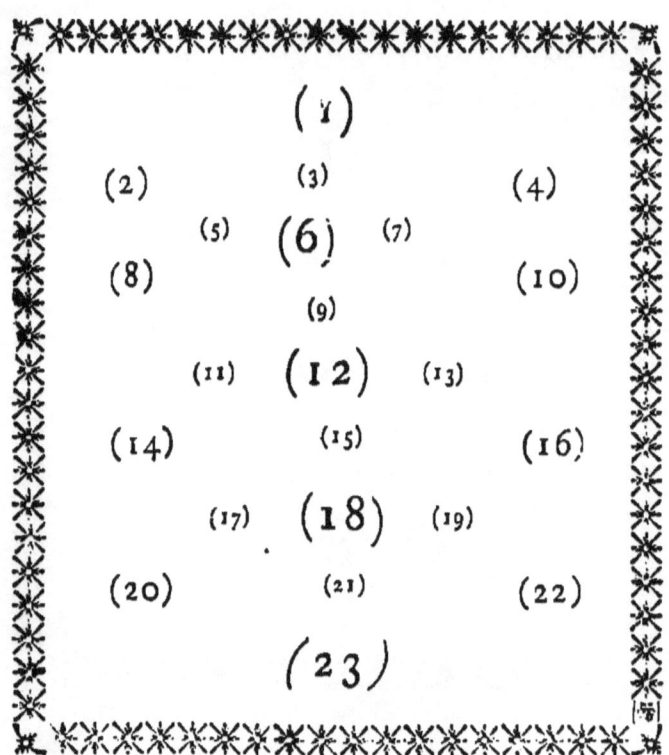

1. A Bret. *Rem.* Turk. Pouts
2. Sweetbreads brown.
3. Hedge-Hog.
4. Boiled Chickens.
5. Cherries.
6. Jellies and Pine-Apple
7. Codlings.
8. Forced Artichokes.
9. Flummery,
10. Green Goose Pye.
11. Sham Melon.
12. Dried Sweetmeats
13. Strawberries
14. A Ham.
15. Curds.
16. Peas.
17. Raspberris.
18. Currant Possets and Pine-Apple.
19. Currant Jelly.
20. Boiled Rabbits.
21. A Trifle.
22. Beef Olives.
23. A Haunch of Venison

A Supper in *July*.

```
                    (1)
      (2)         (3)              (4)
            (5)  (6)  (7)
      (8)                          (10)
                  (9)
            (11) (12) (13)
      (14)       (15)              (16)
            (17) (18) (19)
      (20)       (21)              (22)
                 (23)
```

1 Boiled Chickens
2 Cray Fish
3 Jelly
4 Codling Tart
5 Cherries
6 Currant Poffets
7 Strawberries
8 Peafe
9 Flummery
10 Ducks
11 Gooseberry fool
12 Wet Sweetmeats
13 Chocolate Cream
14 Mutton Maintelow
15 Curls
16 Artichokes
17 Currants
18 Currant Poffets
19 Rafps
20 Cold Tongue
21 Hand of Cards
22 Solomongundy
23 Roaft Rabbets

L

A Dinner in *August*.

FIRST COURSE.

```
            (1)
   (2)     (3)     (4)
   (5)     (6)     (7)
   (8)     (9)    (10)
           (11)
```

1. Stewed Eels.
2. Boiled Chickens.
3. Roots
4. Mutton Collops.
5. Olive Pie.
6. Green Peas Soop.
7. Turkey Pouts larded.
8. Palates white.
9. Currant Jelly.
10. Bacon.
11. A Neck of Venison.

SECOND COURSE.

{1}

{2}   (3)   {4}

{5}   {6}   {7}

{8}   (9)   {10}

{11}

1. Ruffs and Reifs.
2. Orange Poffet.
3. Quince.
4. Sweetmeat Tarts.
5. Collar'd Pig.
6. Cuftard in Egg-Shells.
7. Sturgeon.
8. Almond Cheefe-Cakes.
9. Oranges.
10. Bacon and Eggs made of Flummery.
11. A Guinea-Hen.

A Supper for *August*.

```
            {1}

  {2}      (3)      {4}
  {5}      {6}      {7}
  {8}     [(9)     {10}

            {11}
```

1 Breaſt of Veal ragoo'd white.
2 Peach Tart
3 Quinces
4 Roaſt Pigeons
5 Collar'd Breaſt of Mutton
6 Lemon Poſſets
7 Sturgeon
8 Stew'd Oyſters
9 Damſins
10 Apple Fritters
11 Hare

A Dinner in *September*.

FIRST COURSE.

```
           {1}

   {2}    (3)    {4}

           {5}

   {6}    (7)    {8}

           {9}
```

1 Boiled Turkey
2 Oyſter Loaves
3 Kidney Beans
4 Sham Gooſe
5 Stewed Cucumber
6 Boiled Tongue
7 Colliflower
8 Bumbais
9 Jiggit of Mutton roaſted

SECOND COURSE.

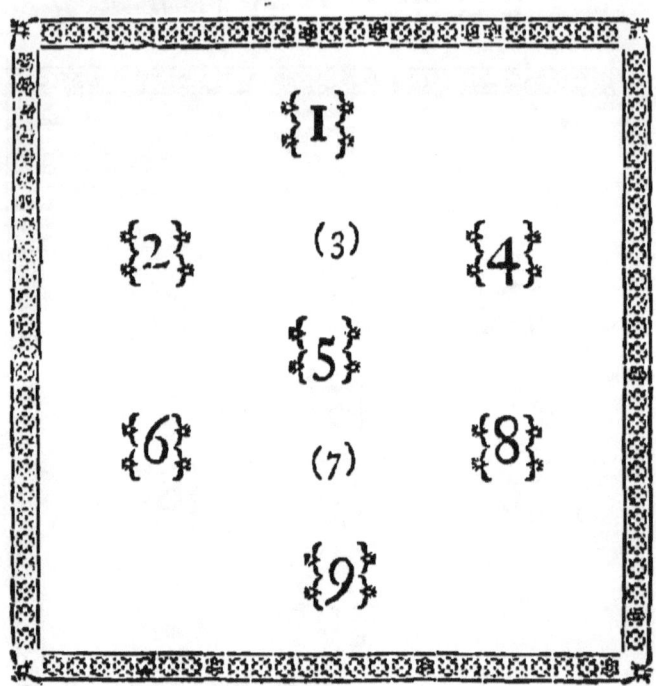

1 Fricasey of Chickens white
2 Partridges roasted
3 Apricots
4 Apple Fritters
5 Neſt or Eggs
6 Stewed Muſhrooms
7 Wine Sours
8 Hot Lobſter
9 Wild Ducks

A Supper in *September*.

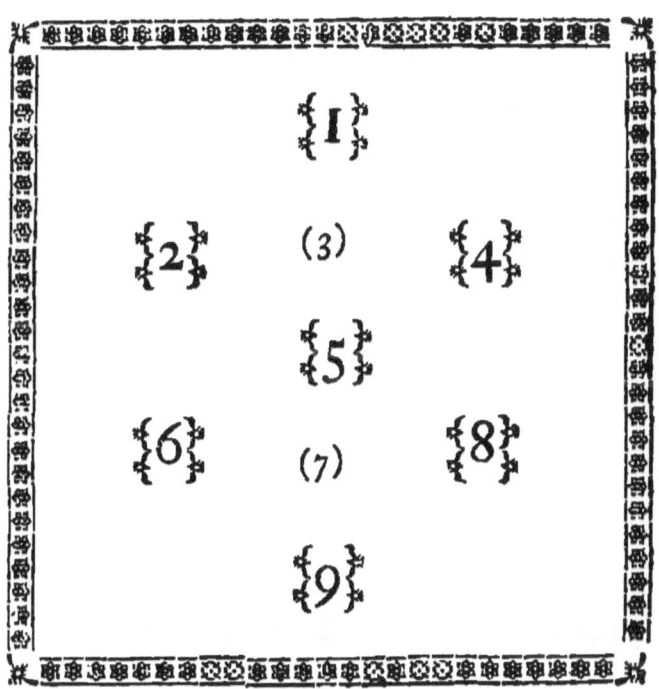

1 Veal in Vale.
2 Boiled Chickens.
3 Green Limes.
4 Broiled Pigeons.
5 Custards in Egg Shells.
6 Escallop'd Oysters.
7 Apricots.
8 Stewed Mushrooms.
9 Turkey Pie.

A Dinner in *October*.

FIRST COURSE.

```
(1)      {2}      (3)

{4}      (5)      {6}

         {7}

{8}      (9)     {10}

(11)    {12}     (13)
```

1. Pudding Sauce.
2. Sham Turtle.
3. Poiverade Sauce.
4. Puddings.
5. Pickles.
6. Mutton Maintelow.
7. Cray Fish Soop
8. Whiteing skinned and broiled.
9. Apple Sauce.
10. Fricasey of Rabbits white.
11. Fish Sauce.
12. Leg of Pork roasted.
13. Butter.

SECOND COURSE.

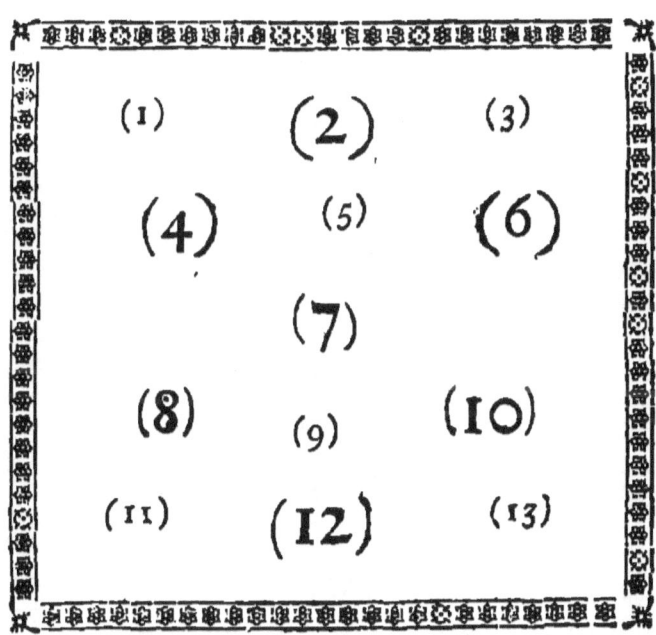

1. Cherries.
2. Moor Game.
3. Green Limes.
4. Minced Pies.
5. Bread Sauce.
6. Plover.
7. Jellies.
8. Snipes.
9. Currant Jelly.
10. Buttered Crab.
11. Apricots.
12. A Hare.
13. Wine Sours.

A Supper in October.

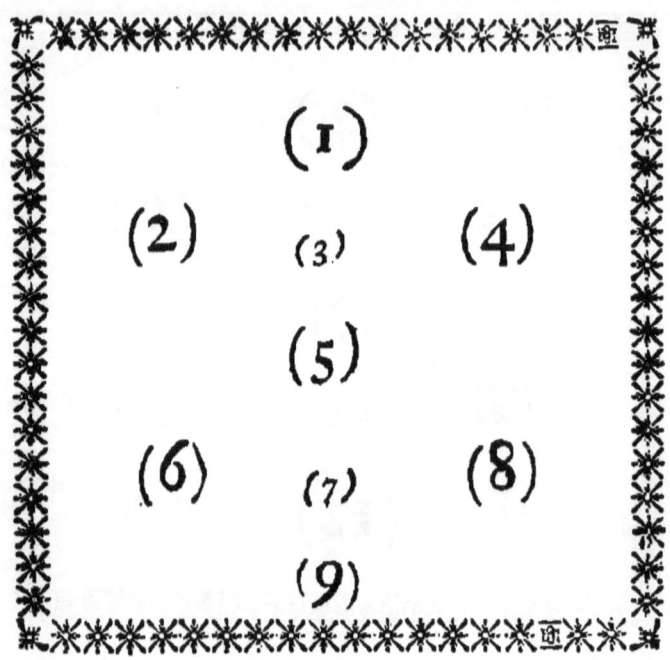

1. Whiteing skinned and broiled.
2. Partridge.
3. Cheese Cakes.
4. Sweet-breads fricasied.
5. Jel y turned out.
6. Mutton Collop.
7. Tarts.
8. Plover.
9. A Hare roasted.

A Dinner in *November*.

FIRST COURSE.

```
            (1)

    (2)    (3)     (4)

           (5)

    (6)            (8)
           (7)

           (9)
```

1. Cod's Head.
2. Veal in Vale.
3. Boat.
4. Boiled Partridges, Sellery Sauce.
5. Cherry Pudding.
6. Escalop'd Oysters.
7. Boat.
8. Breast of Mutton carbonaded.
9. Venison Pasty.

SECOND COURSE.

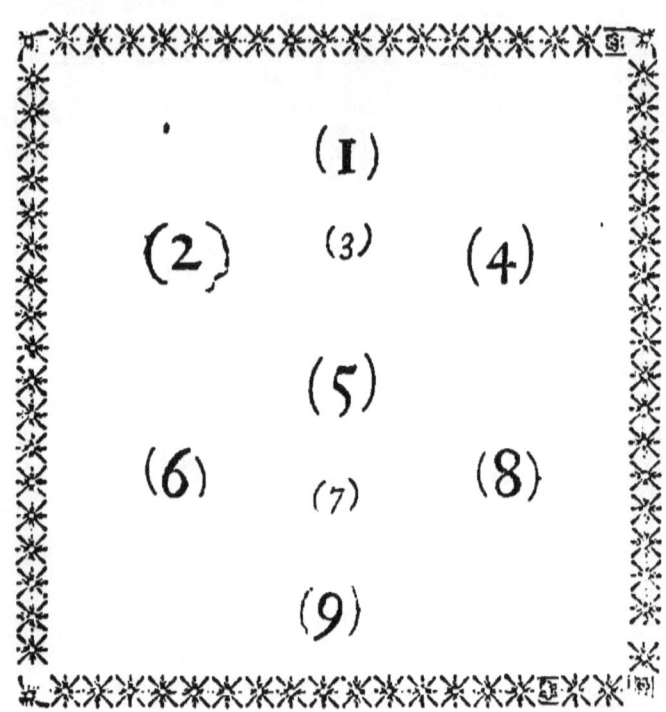

1. Wood Cocks.
2. Solomongundy.
3. Cards.
4. Ambaſſador Cream.
5. Orange Poſſets.
6. Tart.
7. Cuſtard.
8. Collar'd Eels.
9. Teal.

A Supper in *November*.

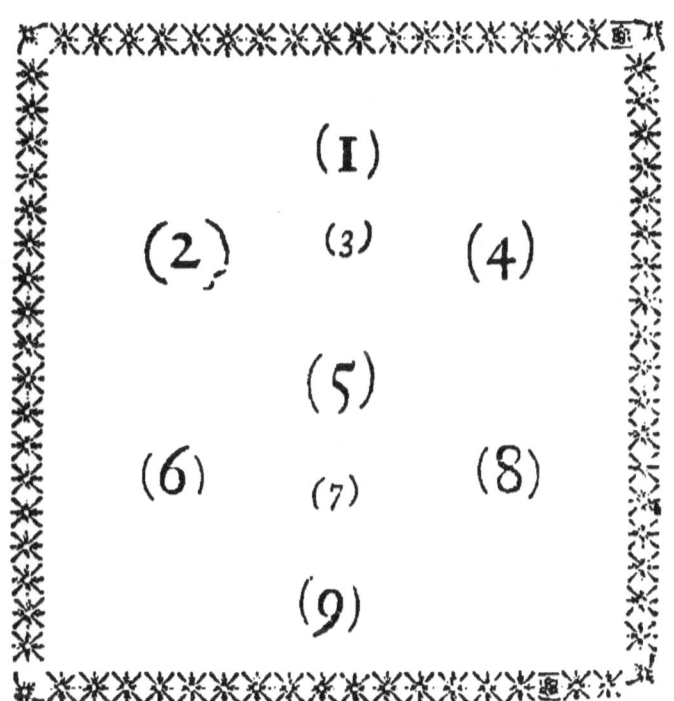

1. Boiled Turkey.
2. Wood Cock.
3. Lemon Cream.
4. Smelts fryed.
5. Orange Pye.
6. Stewed Oysters.
7. Rhenish Cream.
8. Larks.
9. Wild Ducks.

A Dinner in December.

```
                    (1)
      (2)          (3)            (4)
                    (5)
      (6)    (7)   (8)   (9)    (10)
                   (11)
     (12)         (13)           (14)
                (15)  (16)
     (17)         (18)           (19)
                (20)  (21)
                    (22)
     (23)                        (25)
                   (24)
     (26)   (27)  (28)  (29)    (30)
                   (31)
     (32)         (33)           (34)
                   (35)
```

1. Soop Fish. Rem. Pheasant.
2. Boiled Chickens.
3. Games.
4. Sweetbreads.
5. Shrimp.
6. Oyster Loaves.
7. Ambassador Cream.
8. Jellies.
9. Bacon and Eggs.
10. Woodcocks. 11. Winesours.
12. Teal. 13. Cheesecakes.
14. Puddings. 15. Limes.
16. Cherries.
17. Mutton Chops.
18. Dry Sweetmeats.
19. Veal Olives.
20. Damsins. 21. Apricots.
22. Tart. 23. Partridges.
24. Rhenish Cream.
25. Ham. 26. Stewed Pigeons.
27. A Handful of Cards.
28. Jellies. 29. Strawberries.
30. A Turkey. 31. A Trifle.
32. A Hare Pie.
33. Quince. 34. Palates.
35. Soop Fish, Rem. Venison.

A Supper in *December*.

```
                    (1)
  (2)           (3)              (4)
                (5)
  (6)      (7) (8) (9)           (10)
                (11)
  (12)         (13)              (14)
           (15)    (16)
  (17)
                (18)

            (20)   (21)
  (23)          (22)
                (24)
  (26)     (27)(28)(29)          (30)
                (31)
  (32)         (33)              (34)
                (35)
```

1. Boiled Turkey.
2. Woodcocks. 3. Custard.
4. Stewed Oysters.
5. Wine sours. 6. Tansey.
7. Apricots. 8. Posset.
9. Quince. 10. Teal.
11. Walnuts in Sack.
12. Veal Olives.
13. Fricasy of Eggs.
14. Puffs. 15. Sturgeon.
16. Cupid's Hedge-hogs.
17. Sweetmeats. 18. Prunellos.
19. Cold Tongue.
20. Candid Ginger.
21. Pistachoes. 22. Cherries.
23. Fricasey of Chickens white.
24. Hen's Nest. 25. Partridges.
26. A Wild Duck. 27. Greens.
28. Syllabubs. 29. Dumplins.
31. Orange Pye.
32. Cheese-Cakes.
33. Palates. 34. Currant Jelly
35. Snipes.
35. A Neck of Venison.

INDEX.

	Page.
ANCHOVIES to keep	28
Artichoke bottoms to fricasey	88
—— Bottoms to dry	127
—— to boil	128
Apricots to keep	110
—— to preserve green	172
—— to preserve	173
Asparagus to boil	128
Almonds to candy	182
—— Jumbals to make	157
Angelica to candy	181

B

BROTH for a sick person to make	10
—— of mutton	12
Barbets to stew	23
—— to broil	24
Beef rump to stew	37
—— brisket to stew	ibid
—— surloin to force	38
—— round to boil	ibid
—— olives	ibid
—— cakes to dress	39
—— a la mode	ibid
—— Dutch to make	ibid
—— to collar	40
—— to pot	92
Bullocks heart to bake	ibid
Bubble and Squeak to make	91
Beans to boil	129
Barberries to pickle	137
—— to preserve	174
—— drops to make	ibid
Beet root to pickle	138

	Page.
Buns to make	155
Bread, French to make	156
Biscuits, crimson to make	157
Blangt-menge to make	162
Bacon and Eggs	163
Barley Sugar, to make	183
Black caps, to make	184
Brandy Lemon	185
—— black cherry	185
—— ratifia	ibid
Butter to recover	201

C

CODS head to boil	18
—— to crimp	19
—— to stew	ibid
—— zoons to fry	ibid
—— tail to boil	ibid
Carp brown to stew	20
—— white to stew	ibid
—— to broil	ibid
—— to boil	21
Cockles to pickle	27
Crab ham, to make	29
Calf's feet to fry	49
—— feet to collar	50
—— head hash	ibid
Collops Scots to make	51
—— Scots white to make	52
—— Scots chopped to make	ibid
Capons to roast	61
Chickens to boil	64
—— to roast	ibid
—— to force	ibid
Cyder to make	198

Chick-

INDEX.

Chickens to broil	65	Cake seed light	ib'd
—— to fry	ib'd	—— pound	151
—— to fricasey	86	—— icing, for	ibid
—— to fricasey brown	ibid	—— Queen	ibid
Charrs to pot	93	—— little plumb	ib'd
Cramberries keep for tarts	110	—— ginger	152
Cucumbers stewed	125	—— Yarm	153
Cabbage to force	126	—— Shrewsbery	154
—— or sprouts to boil	128	—— sugar	155
—— to pickle white	139	—— bisuit	ibid
—— to pickle red	140	—— common	156
—— to stew red	124	—— to keep all year	ibid
Carrots to boil	129	—— rasphery clear	171
Colliflowers to boil	ibid	Cracknels to make	154
—— to pickle	136	Colouring red to make	157
—— to pickle red	137	—— green to make	158
Coalins to pickle	135	Cupid's hedge hogs	158
—— like mango	ib'd	Cards to make	166
Catchup walnut to make	144	Cherries morella to preserve	
—— mushroom	ibid		173
—— rich	145	—— to dry	1001
Cheese cream to make	145	Codlins to preserve	183
—— sipcoat	ib'd	**D**	
—— Sage	146	DUCKS to roast	65
Cheese Cakes almond	147	—— to boil	66
—— Rice	ibid	Ducklings a-la mode	ib'd
—— curd	148	Ducks wild to do it	75
—— orange	ibid	—— to dress	ibid
Custard almond	148	Dotterels to roast	80
Curds cream	149	Damsins to keep for tarts	109
Cream sagoo	ibid	Damsins to preserve	173
—— lemon	161	Dumplins plumb	110
—— lemon yellow	162	—— drop to make	ibid
—— rhenish	163	—— apple	141
—— chocolate	ibid	**E**	
—— apple	ibid	EELS to boil	21
—— quince	164	—— to stew	22
—— ambassador	ib'd	—— to spitchcock	ibid
Cake plumb	149	—— to collar	23
—— Seed	150		

INDEX.

Eggs, a fricasey of — 87
—— a fricasey white of ibid
—— with indive 89
—— stuffed to make ibid
—— in moonshine to make 90
—— with juice of sorrel ibid
—— with anchovies ibid
—— amblet to make of ibid
—— with spinage 91
Egg to make as large as six
—— ibid
—— to make a nest of 166

F

Flounders to dress — 25
Fish balls to make 32
Fish when in season 34, 35, 36. and 37
Forcemeat balls to make 52
Fowls to boil — 61
—— to broil ibid
—— to roast ibid
—— to boil with jellery 62
—— a-la-braise ibid
—— to hash 63
Figs to keep all the year 110
—— green to preserve 176
—— ripe to preserve ibid
Fritters parsnip to make 130
—— apple ibid
—— drop ibid
—— oatmeal 131
—— royal ibid
—— clarret 132
Force bacon to make ibid
—— oyster or cunele ibid
French to p le 140
Flummery calf's feet 164
—— hartshorn 165

G

GRAVY brown to make 5
—— white 6
Goose ham to make 54
—— to roast 66
—— to boil 67
—— to dry ibid
—— a-la-mode ibid
—— green to roast 68
—— wild to roast 76
—— giblets to stew ibid
Guiney hen to roast 75
Gooseberries keep for tarts 109
—— red to preserve 180
—— to preserve 180
—— fool to make 159
Grapes to keep 110
—— to preserve 179
Gerkins to pickle 138
Ginger bread red 152
—— white 153
—— another ibid
Ginger to candy 181

H

HODGE Podge to make 13
Haddocks to dress 30
Herrings to fry 33
—— to broil ibid
—— to bake 34
Ham to salt 55
Hern to roast 80
Peach Cock to stew ibid
Hare to roast 81
—— with skin on 82
—— to fry ibid
—— to make civet of 83
—— to dress Swiss way ibid
—— jugged ibid
—— potted to make 92
Hog snout to pickle 136
Hedge Hog to make 159

INDEX.

I
JACK to fry 25
Indian pickle to make 141
Jelly calf's foot 168
——— hartshorn ibid
——— ribband ibid
——— cray fish 169
——— currant ibid
——— of pippins 170
——— of bullies ibid
Jam of bullies 171
——— raspberry ibid

K
KIDNEY beans to boil 128
——— to pickle 137

L
LAmpreys to fry 21
——— with sweet
  sauce ibid
Lobsters to pickle 28
——— to roast 29
——— to stew ibid
——— to butter ibid
——— to pot 91
Lamb a jigget to boil 45
——— slices to dress 46
——— stones to fry ibid
——— leg to force ibid
——— purtenance to dress ibid
——— to roast 47
Lapwings to stew 79
Larks to roast 81
——— to dress pear fashion ibid
Leveret to roast 82
Lettice to stew 125
Lemons to preserve 181
Lemonade 180

M
MULLETS to boil 24
——— to broil ibid
Mackarel to boil 32
Muscles to stew ibid
Mutton, a harrico 42
——— leg to force ibid
——— leg to boil ibid
——— loin to boil 43
——— a breast to carbonade ib
——— kebobed ibid
——— maintelow ibid
——— rumps to dress 44
——— collops ibid
——— leg to dry 45
——— a breast to collar ibid
——— a chine, or saddle to
  roast ibid
Mooregame to roast 75
——— to pot 95
Mushrooms a fricasey of 88
——— to pot 94
——— to stew 125
——— to pickle 134
——— powder to make 144
Mulberries to keep 110
Mackaroons, French to make 123
——— another way 156
Mellons to pickle 138
——— to make 167
Medlars to preserve 180
Mead strong 195
——— small 196
Meat rules for roasting and
  boiling 200

O
OYSTERS to stew 31
——— loaves to make ibid
——— to escalop ibid
——— to pickle 32
——— to fry ibid

INDEX.

Ox check to bake	40
—— palates to dress	41
Ortolans roasted	76
—————— fryed ——	ibid
Onions to pickle	139
—————— Spanish to pickle	ibid
Oranges to preserve	174
—————— chips to candy	182
Orgeat to make	187

P

POTTAGE to make with herbs	14
Pike to roast ——	24
—— to boil ——	25
Plaice to stew	26
—— to fry	ibid
Prawns to stew	33
Pullow to make	54
Pork mittoon ——	53
—— griskins to make	55
—— leg to roast	ibid
—— potted to make	93
Pigs head to collar	ibid
—— feet and ears to dress	56
—— feet and ears to fricasey ——	87
Pig to roast ——	56
—— to boil ——	57
—— to fricasey	88
Pullets roasted	62
—————— surprize to make	63
Pigeons to roast	68
—— to boil	69
—— palpatoon to make	ibid
—— to broil whole	ibid
—— transmogrified	ibid
—— in a hole	70
—— to jugg	ibid
—— to grill	ibid
—— stoved to make	71
—— in surtout	ibid
—— to pickle	72
Partridges to roast	ibid
—— to boil	ibid
—— young, with oysters	73
—— hash to make	ibid
Pheasant to roast	ibid
—— to boil	ibid
—— to stew	74
Peacock to boil	ibid
Plover to roast	78
—— to capurine	ibid
Paste for a pasty to make	96
—— for a goose pye	ibid
—— for tarts	ibid
—— shell to make	97
—— to wash the hands	107
Puss	99
Pye orange to make	97
—— calf's foot to make	98
—— hare to make	99
—— Turkey to make	ibid
—— pigeon to make	100
—— turbots head to make	ibid
—— eel to make	ibid
—— young rook to make	ibid
—— Olive	101
—— rabbet ——	ibid
—— oyster	ibid
—— lobster	102
—— an umble	ibid
—— beef stake	103
Perry to make	198

INDEX.

Pye green goose	ibid	Pudding quince	ibid
—— swan	ibid	—— plumb cake	ibid
—— pheasant	ibid	—— a beggar's	ibid
—— fawn	104	—— rye bread	117
—— Yorkshire Christmas	ibid	—— pippin	ibid
		—— herb	ibid
—— goose	105	—— custard	ibid
—— bride	ibid	—— oatmeal	118
—— lark	106	—— of different colours	ibid
—— calf's chaldron	ibid		
—— calf's head	ibid	—— a stake	ibid
—— apple	ibid	—— in skins	119
—— minced	107	—— black in skins	ibid
—— ham	108	—— white in skins	ibid
—— chicken	ibid	Pancakes, called a quire of paper	121
—— egg	ibid		
Pasty venison to make	102	—— clary	ibid
—— beef	107	—— cream	122
Patties to make	108	—— royal	ibid
Peaches and plumbs to keep	110	—— rice	ibid
		Pears to stew	124
Pudding rice to make	111	—— or pippins to dry	127
—— carrot	ibid	Parsnips to stew	125
—— orange	ibid	Pease to stew	127
—— calf's foot	112	Posset sack	160
—— marrow	ibid	—— orange	ibid
—— gooseberry	113	—— lemon	ibid
—— raspberry	ibid	—— currant	161
—— apple	ibid	Pear plumbs white to preserve	177
—— millet	ibid		
—— hunting	114	Plumbs amber yellow to preserve	179
—— apricot	ibid		
—— ratifia	ibid	Peaches in brandy	180
—— potatoe	ibid	Pippins golden to preserve	183
—— quaking	115		
—— lemon	ibid		
—— almond	ibid	QUAILS to roast	77
—— wine	116	Quinces to preserve	175
		—— white	176

Rasp-

INDEX.

R
Raspberries to preserve 171
——— to keep 110
——— fool to make 171
Ruddock to dress 75
——— ibid
Ruffs and reifs to dress 76
Raises to boil 79
Rabbets to roast 84
——— to boil ibid
——— to dress like moor-game ibid
——— to dress with bacon 85
——— pulled to make ibid
——— to stew the French way ibid
——— a fricasey of ibid
——— ditto white of 86
——— to pot 94
Raddish buds to pickle 140
Rules to be observed in pickling 142
Ramakins to make 146
Rabbets scotch to make ibid
——— portugal ibid
——— Italian 147

S
Soop vermicelli to make 6
——— onion ibid
——— cray fish 7
——— green peafe ibid
——— hare 8
——— cucumber ibid
——— gravy ibid
——— almond 9
——— rice ibid
——— veal with barley ibid
——— mushroom 10
——— meagre ibid
——— peafe for Lent ibid
——— for pocket 11
——— cake of beef 12
——— calf's head ibid
——— oyster ibid
——— without water 13
Salmon to dress 14
——— to roast whole ibid
——— jole to boil 15
——— to fry ibid
——— to pickle ibid
——— to stew 16
——— in cases ibid
——— to pot as at New-castle 93
Scate to crimp 25
Soals to fry 26
——— to boil 28
Sturgeon to pickle 26
Sprats to pickle 27
Soockey water to make 30
Shrimps to escalop 33
Sausages pork to make 57
——— Bolognia ibid
Snipes to roast 77
Sweet breads to fricasey 87
Skirrets to fricasey 89
Strawberries to keep 110
Solomangundy to make 123
——— transparent ibid
Sellery stewed 125
Sel-

INDI

Sellery to pickle 140	Turkey po..
Spinage to stew 126	Thrushes to r...
Sprouts or cabbage to boil 128	Teal to roast
Samphire to pickle 136	—— to boil
Syllabubs to make 161	—— to roast with olī
Skennel 164	Tarts in glasses to ma—
Sugar to know when candy height 183	—— another way ib —— gooseberry 16.
Shrub to make 184	Tansey to make 12...
Syrrup of lemons 184	Tarragon to pickle 142
—— of mulberries 185	Trifle to make 149
—— of cowslips ibid	Tarts of different Sorts to make 199
—— of violets 186	
Surfeit water to make 196	**U**

T

TURBOT to boil 17	VEAL, a breast to ragoo 47
—— to fry ibid	—— ditto, white ibid
—— to souse ibid	—— breast to roast 48
—— infant to dress 18	—— in vale ibid
—— to bake ibid	—— sweet breads to fry ib.
Tench to boil 22	—— Blanquet 49
—— to stew 23	—— fillet to stuff and roast ibid
—— to bake ibid	—— cutlets to make ibid
Trout to fry 30	—— olives to make 52
—— to p... ibid	—— aladab to make 53
—— to pot 94	—— bur... ditto ibid
—— sour to dress 129	—— potted 95
Tongues to pickle 41	Venison to rec... ... 58
—— neats to roast ibid	—— haunch to ... ...
—— calf to boil 54	—— neck to roast ib...
Turtle sham to make 51	—— to pot 92
Tripe to fry 58	Vinegar gooseberry to mak: 142
—— fricasey white 59	—— elder 143
—— fricasey brown 87	—— raisin ibid
Turkey to roast ibid	—— sugar ibid
—— to boil ibid	Verjuice to make 199
—— pulled to make 60	Wood.
—— a-la-daube ibid	

INDEX.

—	76	Wine birch	ibid
pot	95	— elder	ibid
...ench way	77	— cherry	191
...er	132	— balm	191
make	133	— currantberry white	
...tch	ibid		192
...to pickle	134	— apricot	ibid
— to pickle green	ibid	— sage	193
— to pickle white	136	— damsin	ibid
Wiggs to make	154	— quince	194
Windsor poor knights	155	— mulberry	ibid
Wine sours to preserve	177	— blackberry	ibid
— orange	187	— elder flower	195
— cowslip	188	— gilliflower	ibid
— gooseberries	ibid	Water Barbadoes to make	197
— currantberry	189	— Plague ditto	ibid
— raisin	190	Water Tar to make	198

www.ingramcontent.com/pod-product-compliance
Lightning Source LLC
Chambersburg PA
CBHW031740230426
43669CB00007B/417